OXFORD STUDENT TEXTS

Series Editor: Nid Lee

*

W. B. Yeats
Selected Poems

*

Edited by Richard Gill Withdrawn

Oxford University Press
1993

for Miriam and Naomi

Oxford University Press, Walton Street, Oxford OX2 6DP

Oxford New York Toronto
Delhi Bombay Calcutta Madras Karachi
Kuala Lumpur Singapore Hong Kong Tokyo
Nairobi Dar es Salaam Cape Town
Melbourne Auckland Madrid
and associated companies in
Berlin Ibadan

Oxford is a trade mark of Oxford University Press

First published by Oxford University Press

ISBN 0 19 831966 5

Typeset by Pentacor PLC, High Wycombe, Bucks
Printed and bound in Great Britain by
Butler & Tanner Ltd, Frome and London

The publishers would like to thank the following for permission to
reproduce photographs:

Hulton Deutsch Collection Ltd p.143; Irish Tourist Board p.146 a),
p.147; Mansell Collection Ltd p.146 b); National Library of Ireland
p.144, p.145; National Portrait Gallery, London p.148.

The cover illustration is by Susan Scott

Contents

Acknowledgements

Unlike some of the people who may use this book, I have never studied Yeats as part of an examination course. Consequently, I have no teachers to thank for leading me through this body of invigorating poetry. But like many readers of Yeats, I have met people, whose enthusiasm has encouraged me to read him. In this respect, I remember Marion Shaw of Hull University, who spoke warmly of her appreciation of Yeats' language. I would also like to record my thanks to Jill Burbidge, Bela Gor, Lucy Hooper, Victor Lee, Patricia MacLachlan, and Caroline Mardall. I have used the Macmillan text for the poems.

Richard Gill

Editors

Dr Victor Lee

Victor Lee, the series editor, read English at University College, Cardiff. He was later awarded his doctorate at the University of Oxford. He has taught at secondary and tertiary level, and is currently working at the Open University. There, he has been involved in the making of a considerable number of texts, television and radio programmes. Victor Lee's experience as an examiner is very wide: he has been a Chief Examiner in English at A-level for three different boards stretching over a period of twenty years.

Richard Gill

Richard Gill read English and Theology at Hull University, followed by an M.A. in Victorian Literature at Leicester. He has taught at school, F.E., Poly, and University level. Currently, he is Head of English at Wyggeston and Queen Elizabeth I College, Leicester.

He has edited *Donne: Selected Poems* in the Oxford Student Texts series and has written a book on Tennyson's *In Memoriam*, as well as a general introduction to the study of Literature. He is an experienced A-level examiner and has frequently broadcast on historical and literary topics.

Foreword

Oxford Student Texts are specifically aimed at presenting poetry and drama to an audience which is studying English Literature at an advanced level. Each text is designed as an integrated whole consisting of three main parts. The poetry or the play is always placed first to stress its importance and to encourage students to enjoy it without secondary critical material of any kind. When help is needed on other occasions, the second and third parts of these texts, the Notes and the Approaches, provide it.

The Notes perform two functions. First, they provide information and explain allusions. Secondly, and this is where they differ from most texts at this level, they often raise questions of central concern to the interpretation of the poem or the play being dealt with, particularly in the use of a general note placed at the beginning of the particular notes.

The third part, the Approaches section, deals with major issues of response to the particular selection of poetry or drama, as opposed to the work of the writer as a whole. One of the major aims of this part of the text is to emphasize that there is no one right answer to interpretation, but a series of approaches. Readers are given guidance as to what counts as evidence, but, in the end, left to make up their minds as to which are the most suitable interpretations, or to add their own.

To help achieve this, the Approaches section contains a number of activity-discussion sequences, although it must be stressed that these are optional. Significant issues about the poetry or the play are raised in these activities. Readers are invited to tackle these activities before proceeding to the discussion section where possible responses to the questions raised in the activities are considered. Their main function is to engage readers actively in the ideas of the text. However, these activity-discussion sequences are so arranged that, if readers wish to treat the Approaches as continuous prose and not attempt the activities, they can.

At the end of each text there is also a list of Tasks. Whereas the activity-discussion sequences are aimed at increasing understanding of the literary work itself, these tasks are intended to help explore ideas about the poetry or the play after the student has completed the reading of the work and the studying of the Notes and Approaches. These tasks are particularly helpful for coursework projects or in preparing for an examination.

Victor Lee   Series Editor

The Poems

from *Crossways*

Down by the Salley Gardens

Down by the salley gardens my love and I did meet;
She passed the salley gardens with little snow-white feet.
She bid me take love easy, as the leaves grow on the
    tree;
But I, being young and foolish, with her would not
    agree.

In a field by the river my love and I did stand,
And on my leaning shoulder she laid her snow-white
    hand.
She bid me take life easy, as the grass grows on the weirs;
But I was young and foolish, and now am full of tears.

from *The Rose*

The Lake Isle of Innisfree

I will arise and go now, and go to Innisfree,
And a small cabin build there, of clay and wattles made:
Nine bean-rows will I have there, a hive for the honey-
    bee,
And live alone in the bee-loud glade.

And I shall have some peace there, for peace comes
    dropping slow,
Dropping from the veils of the morning to where the
    cricket sings;
There midnight's all a glimmer, and noon a purple glow,
And evening full of the linnet's wings.

I will arise and go now, for always night and day
10 I hear lake water lapping with low sounds by the shore;
While I stand on the roadway, or on the pavements grey,
I hear it in the deep heart's core.

When You Are Old

When you are old and grey and full of sleep,
And nodding by the fire, take down this book,
And slowly read, and dream of the soft look
Your eyes had once, and of their shadows deep;

How many loved your moments of glad grace,
And loved your beauty with love false or true,
But one man loved the pilgrim soul in you,
And loved the sorrows of your changing face;

And bending down beside the glowing bars,
10 Murmur, a little sadly, how Love fled
And paced upon the mountains overhead
And hid his face amid a crowd of stars.

from *The Wind Among the Reeds*

He Wishes for the Cloths of Heaven

Had I the heavens' embroidered cloths,
Enwrought with golden and silver light,
The blue and the dim and the dark cloths
Of night and light and the half-light,
I would spread the cloths under your feet:
But I, being poor, have only my dreams;
I have spread my dreams under your feet;
Tread softly because you tread on my dreams.

from *In the Seven Woods*

Adam's Curse

We sat together at one summer's end,
That beautiful mild woman, your close friend,
And you and I, and talked of poetry.
I said, 'A line will take us hours maybe;
Yet if it does not seem a moment's thought,
Our stitching and unstitching has been naught.
Better go down upon your marrow-bones
And scrub a kitchen pavement, or break stones
Like an old pauper, in all kinds of weather;
10 For to articulate sweet sounds together
Is to work harder than all these, and yet
Be thought an idler by the noisy set
Of bankers, schoolmasters, and clergymen
The martyrs call the world.'

                  And thereupon
That beautiful mild woman for whose sake
There's many a one shall find out all heartache
On finding that her voice is sweet and low
Replied, 'To be born woman is to know—
Although they do not talk of it at school—
20 That we must labour to be beautiful.'

I said, 'It's certain there is no fine thing
Since Adam's fall but needs much labouring.
There have been lovers who thought love should be
So much compounded of high courtesy
That they would sigh and quote with learned looks
Precedents out of beautiful old books;
Yet now it seems an idle trade enough.'

We sat grown quiet at the name of love;
We saw the last embers of daylight die,
30 And in the trembling blue-green of the sky
A moon, worn as if it had been a shell
Washed by time's waters as they rose and fell
About the stars and broke in days and years.

I had a thought for no one's but your ears:
That you were beautiful, and that I strove
To love you in the old high way of love;
That it had all seemed happy, and yet we'd grown
As weary-hearted as that hollow moon.

from *The Green Helmet and Other Poems*

No Second Troy

Why should I blame her that she filled my days
With misery, or that she would of late
Have taught to ignorant men most violent ways,
Or hurled the little streets upon the great,
Had they but courage equal to desire?
What could have made her peaceful with a mind
That nobleness made simple as a fire,
With beauty like a tightened bow, a kind
That is not natural in an age like this,
10 Being high and solitary and most stern?
Why, what could she have done, being what she is?
Was there another Troy for her to burn?

The Mask

'Put off that mask of burning gold
With emerald eyes.'
'O no, my dear, you make so bold
To find if hearts be wild and wise,
And yet not cold.'

'I would but find what's there to find,
Love or deceit.'
'It was the mask engaged your mind,
And after set your heart to beat,
10 Not what's behind.'

'But lest you are my enemy,
I must enquire.'
'O no, my dear, let all that be;
What matter, so there is but fire
In you, in me?'

from *Responsibilities*

'Pardon, Old Fathers'

Pardon, old fathers, if you still remain
Somewhere in ear-shot for the story's end,
Old Dublin merchant 'free of the ten and four'
Or trading out of Galway into Spain;
Old country scholar, Robert Emmet's friend,
A hundred-year-old memory to the poor;
Merchant and scholar who have left me blood
That has not passed through any huckster's loin,
Soldiers that gave, whatever die was cast:
10   A Butler or an Armstrong that withstood
Beside the brackish waters of the Boyne
James and his Irish when the Dutchman crossed;
Old merchant skipper that leaped overboard
After a ragged hat in Biscay Bay;
You most of all, silent and fierce old man,
Because the daily spectacle that stirred
My fancy, and set my boyish lips to say,
'Only the wasteful virtues earn the sun';
Pardon that for a barren passion's sake,
20   Although I have come close on forty-nine,
I have no child, I have nothing but a book,
Nothing but that to prove your blood and mine.

September 1913

What need you, being come to sense,
But fumble in a greasy till
And add the halfpence to the pence
And prayer to shivering prayer, until
You have dried the marrow from the bone?
For men were born to pray and save:
Romantic Ireland's dead and gone,
It's with O'Leary in the grave.

Yet they were of a different kind,
10 The names that stilled your childish play,
They have gone about the world like wind,
But little time had they to pray
For whom the hangman's rope was spun,
And what, God help us, could they save?
Romantic Ireland's dead and gone,
It's with O'Leary in the grave.

Was it for this the wild geese spread
The grey wing upon every tide;
For this that all that blood was shed,
20 For this Edward Fitzgerald died,
And Robert Emmet and Wolfe Tone,
All that delirium of the brave?
Romantic Ireland's dead and gone,
It's with O'Leary in the grave.

Yet could we turn the years again,
And call those exiles as they were
In all their loneliness and pain,
You'd cry, 'Some woman's yellow hair
Has maddened every mother's son':
30 They weighed so lightly what they gave.
But let them be, they're dead and gone,
They're with O'Leary in the grave.

The Cold Heaven

Suddenly I saw the cold and rook-delighting heaven
That seemed as though ice burned and was but the more
    ice,
And thereupon imagination and heart were driven
So wild that every casual thought of that and this
Vanished, and left but memories, that should be out of
    season
With the hot blood of youth, of love crossed long ago;
And I took all the blame out of all sense and reason,
Until I cried and trembled and rocked to and fro,
Riddled with light. Ah! when the ghost begins to
    quicken,
10 Confusion of the death-bed over, it is sent
Out naked on the roads, as the books say, and stricken
By the injustice of the skies for punishment?

The Magi

Now as at all times I can see in the mind's eye,
In their stiff, painted clothes, the pale unsatisfied ones
Appear and disappear in the blue depth of the sky
With all their ancient faces like rain-beaten stones,
And all their helms of silver hovering side by side,
And all their eyes still fixed, hoping to find once more,
Being by Calvary's turbulence unsatisfied,
The uncontrollable mystery on the bestial floor.

A Coat

I made my song a coat
Covered with embroideries
Out of old mythologies
From heel to throat;
But the fools caught it,
Wore it in the world's eyes
As though they'd wrought it.
Song, let them take it,
For there's more enterprise
10 In walking naked.

from *The Wild Swans at Coole*

The Wild Swans at Coole

The trees are in their autumn beauty,
The woodland paths are dry,
Under the October twilight the water
Mirrors a still sky;
Upon the brimming water among the stones
Are nine-and-fifty swans.

The nineteenth autumn has come upon me
Since I first made my count;
I saw, before I had well finished,
10 All suddenly mount
And scatter wheeling in great broken rings
Upon their clamorous wings.

I have looked upon those brilliant creatures,
And now my heart is sore.
All's changed since I, hearing at twilight,
The first time on this shore,
The bell-beat of their wings above my head,
Trod with a lighter tread.

Unwearied still, lover by lover,
20 They paddle in the cold
Companionable streams or climb the air;
Their hearts have not grown old;
Passion or conquest, wander where they will,
Attend upon them still.

But now they drift on the still water,
Mysterious, beautiful;
Among what rushes will they build,

By what lake's edge or pool
Delight men's eyes when I awake some day
30   To find they have flown away?

In Memory of Major Robert Gregory

I

Now that we're almost settled in our house
I'll name the friends that cannot sup with us
Beside a fire of turf in th' ancient tower,
And having talked to some late hour
Climb up the narrow winding stair to bed:
Discoverers of forgotten truth
Or mere companions of my youth,
All, all are in my thoughts tonight being dead.

II

Always we'd have the new friend meet the old
10   And we are hurt if either friend seem cold,
And there is salt to lengthen out the smart
In the affections of our heart,
And quarrels are blown up upon that head;
But not a friend that I would bring
This night can set us quarrelling,
For all that come into my mind are dead.

III

Lionel Johnson comes the first to mind,
That loved his learning better than mankind,
Though courteous to the worst; much falling he
20   Brooded upon sanctity
Till all his Greek and Latin learning seemed
A long blast upon the horn that brought
A little nearer to his thought
A measureless consummation that he dreamed.

IV

And that enquiring man John Synge comes next,
That dying chose the living world for text
And never could have rested in the tomb
But that, long travelling, he had come
Towards nightfall upon certain set apart
30 In a most desolate stony place,
Towards nightfall upon a race
Passionate and simple like his heart.

V

And then I think of old George Pollexfen,
In muscular youth well known to Mayo men
For horsemanship at meets or at racecourses,
That could have shown how pure-bred horses
And solid men, for all their passion, live
But as the outrageous stars incline
By opposition, square and trine;
40 Having grown sluggish and contemplative.

VI

They were my close companions many a year,
A portion of my mind and life, as it were,
And now their breathless faces seem to look
Out of some old picture-book;
I am accustomed to their lack of breath,
But not that my dear friend's dear son,
Our Sidney and our perfect man,
Could share in that discourtesy of death.

VII

For all things the delighted eye now sees
50 Were loved by him: the old storm-broken trees
That cast their shadows upon road and bridge;
The tower set on the stream's edge;

The ford where drinking cattle make a stir
Nightly, and startled by that sound
The water-hen must change her ground;
He might have been your heartiest welcomer.

VIII

When with the Galway foxhounds he would ride
From Castle Taylor to the Roxborough side
Or Esserkelly plain, few kept his pace;
60   At Mooneen he had leaped a place
So perilous that half the astonished meet
Had shut their eyes; and where was it
He rode a race without a bit?
And yet his mind outran the horses' feet.

IX

We dreamed that a great painter had been born
To cold Clare rock and Galway rock and thorn,
To that stern colour and that delicate line
That are our secret discipline
Wherein the gazing heart doubles her might.
70   Soldier, scholar, horseman, he,
And yet he had the intensity
To have published all to be a world's delight.

X

What other could so well have counselled us
In all lovely intricacies of a house
As he that practised or that understood
All work in metal or in wood,
In moulded plaster or in carven stone?
Soldier, scholar, horseman, he,
And all he did done perfectly
80   As though he had but that one trade alone.

XI

Some burn damp faggots, others may consume
The entire combustible world in one small room
As though dried straw, and if we turn about
The bare chimney is gone black out
Because the work had finished in that flare.
Soldier, scholar, horseman, he,
As 'twere all life's epitome.
What made us dream that he could comb grey hair?

XII

I had thought, seeing how bitter is that wind
90 That shakes the shutter, to have brought to mind
All those that manhood tried, or childhood loved
Or boyish intellect approved,
With some appropriate commentary on each;
Until imagination brought
A fitter welcome; but a thought
Of that late death took all my heart for speech.

An Irish Airman Foresees His Death

I know that I shall meet my fate
Somewhere among the clouds above;
Those that I fight I do not hate,
Those that I guard I do not love;
My country is Kiltartan Cross,
My countrymen Kiltartan's poor,
No likely end could bring them loss
Or leave them happier than before.
Nor law, nor duty bade me fight,
10 Nor public men, nor cheering crowds,
A lonely impulse of delight
Drove to this tumult in the clouds;
I balanced all, brought all to mind,
The years to come seemed waste of breath,
A waste of breath the years behind
In balance with this life, this death.

The Living Beauty

I bade, because the wick and oil are spent
And frozen are the channels of the blood,
My discontented heart to draw content
From beauty that is cast out of a mould
In bronze, or that in dazzling marble appears,
Appears, but when we have gone is gone again,
Being more indifferent to our solitude
Than 'twere an apparition. O heart, we are old;
The living beauty is for younger men:
10 We cannot pay its tribute of wild tears.

To a Young Girl

My dear, my dear, I know
More than another
What makes your heart beat so;
Not even your own mother
Can know it as I know,
Who broke my heart for her
When the wild thought,
That she denies
And has forgot,
10   Set all her blood astir
And glittered in her eyes.

The Fisherman

Although I can see him still,
The freckled man who goes
To a grey place on a hill
In grey Connemara clothes
At dawn to cast his flies,
It's long since I began
To call up to the eyes
This wise and simple man.
All day I'd looked in the face
10   What I had hoped 'twould be
To write for my own race
And the reality;
The living men that I hate,
The dead man that I loved,
The craven man in his seat,
The insolent unreproved,
And no knave brought to book
Who has won a drunken cheer,

The witty man and his joke
20 Aimed at the commonest ear,
The clever man who cries
The catch-cries of the clown,
The beating down of the wise
And great Art beaten down.

Maybe a twelvemonth since
Suddenly I began,
In scorn of this audience,
Imagining a man,
And his sun-freckled face,
30 And grey Connemara cloth,
Climbing up to a place
Where stone is dark under froth,
And the down-turn of his wrist
When the flies drop in the stream;
A man who does not exist,
A man who is but a dream;
And cried, 'Before I am old
I shall have written him one
Poem maybe as cold
40 And passionate as the dawn.'

The People

'What have I earned for all that work,' I said,
'For all that I have done at my own charge?
The daily spite of this unmannerly town,
Where who has served the most is most defamed,
The reputation of his lifetime lost
Between the night and morning. I might have lived,
And you know well how great the longing has been,
Where every day my footfall should have lit

In the green shadow of Ferrara wall;
10 Or climbed among the images of the past—
The unperturbed and courtly images—
Evening and morning, the steep street of Urbino
To where the Duchess and her people talked
The stately midnight through until they stood
In their great window looking at the dawn;
I might have had no friend that could not mix
Courtesy and passion into one like those
That saw the wicks grow yellow in the dawn;
I might have used the one substantial right
20 My trade allows: chosen my company,
And chosen what scenery had pleased me best.'
Thereon my phoenix answered in reproof,
'The drunkards, pilferers of public funds,
All the dishonest crowd I had driven away,
When my luck changed and they dared meet my face,
Crawled from obscurity, and set upon me
Those I had served and some that I had fed;
Yet never have I, now nor any time,
Complained of the people.'

                                All I could reply
30 Was: 'You, that have not lived in thought but deed,
Can have the purity of a natural force,
But I, whose virtues are the definitions
Of the analytic mind, can neither close
The eye of the mind nor keep my tongue from speech.'
And yet, because my heart leaped at her words,
I was abashed, and now they come to mind
After nine years, I sink my head abashed.

A Deep-Sworn Vow

Others because you did not keep
That deep-sworn vow have been friends of mine;
Yet always when I look death in the face,
When I clamber to the heights of sleep,
Or when I grow excited with wine,
Suddenly I meet your face.

from *Michael Robartes and The Dancer*

Easter 1916

I have met them at close of day
Coming with vivid faces
From counter or desk among grey
Eighteenth-century houses.
I have passed with a nod of the head
Or polite meaningless words,
Or have lingered awhile and said
Polite meaningless words,
And thought before I had done
10 Of a mocking tale or a gibe
To please a companion
Around the fire at the club,
Being certain that they and I
But lived where motley is worn:
All changed, changed utterly:
A terrible beauty is born.

That woman's days were spent
In ignorant good-will,
Her nights in argument
20 Until her voice grew shrill.
What voice more sweet than hers
When, young and beautiful,
She rode to harriers?
This man had kept a school
And rode our wingèd horse;
This other his helper and friend
Was coming into his force;
He might have won fame in the end,

So sensitive his nature seemed,
30 So daring and sweet his thought.
This other man I had dreamed
A drunken, vainglorious lout.
He had done most bitter wrong
To some who are near my heart,
Yet I number him in the song;
He, too, has resigned his part
In the casual comedy;
He, too, has been changed in his turn,
Transformed utterly:
40 A terrible beauty is born.

Hearts with one purpose alone
Through summer and winter seem
Enchanted to a stone
To trouble the living stream.
The horse that comes from the road,
The rider, the birds that range
From cloud to tumbling cloud,
Minute by minute they change;
A shadow of cloud on the stream
50 Changes minute by minute;
A horse-hoof slides on the brim,
And a horse plashes within it;
The long-legged moor-hens dive,
And hens to moor-cocks call;
Minute by minute they live:
The stone's in the midst of all.

Too long a sacrifice
Can make a stone of the heart.
O when may it suffice?
60 That is Heaven's part, our part
To murmur name upon name,

As a mother names her child
When sleep at last has come
On limbs that had run wild.
What is it but nightfall?
No, no, not night but death;
Was it needless death after all?
For England may keep faith
For all that is done and said.
70 We know their dream; enough
To know they dreamed and are dead;
And what if excess of love
Bewildered them till they died?
I write it out in a verse—
MacDonagh and MacBride
And Connolly and Pearse
Now and in time to be,
Wherever green is worn,
Are changed, changed utterly:
80 A terrible beauty is born.

September 25, 1916

Sixteen Dead Men

O but we talked at large before
The sixteen men were shot,
But who can talk of give and take,
What should be and what not
While those dead men are loitering there
To stir the boiling pot?

You say that we should still the land
Till Germany's overcome;
But who is there to argue that

10   Now Pearse is deaf and dumb?
      And is their logic to outweigh
      MacDonagh's bony thumb?

      How could you dream they'd listen
      That have an ear alone
      For those new comrades they have found,
      Lord Edward and Wolfe Tone,
      Or meddle with our give and take
      That converse bone to bone?

The Second Coming

      Turning and turning in the widening gyre
      The falcon cannot hear the falconer;
      Things fall apart; the centre cannot hold;
      Mere anarchy is loosed upon the world,
      The blood-dimmed tide is loosed, and everywhere
      The ceremony of innocence is drowned;
      The best lack all conviction, while the worst
      Are full of passionate intensity.

      Surely some revelation is at hand;
10   Surely the Second Coming is at hand.
      The Second Coming! Hardly are those words out
      When a vast image out of *Spiritus Mundi*
      Troubles my sight: somewhere in sands of the desert
      A shape with lion body and the head of a man,
      A gaze blank and pitiless as the sun,
      Is moving its slow thighs, while all about it
      Reel shadows of the indignant desert birds.
      The darkness drops again; but now I know
      That twenty centuries of stony sleep
20   Were vexed to nightmare by a rocking cradle,
      And what rough beast, its hour come round at last,
      Slouches towards Bethlehem to be born?

A Prayer for My Daughter

Once more the storm is howling, and half hid
Under this cradle-hood and coverlid
My child sleeps on. There is no obstacle
But Gregory's wood and one bare hill
Whereby the haystack- and roof-levelling wind,
Bred on the Atlantic, can be stayed;
And for an hour I have walked and prayed
Because of the great gloom that is in my mind.

I have walked and prayed for this young child an hour
10 And heard the sea-wind scream upon the tower,
And under the arches of the bridge, and scream
In the elms above the flooded stream;
Imagining in excited reverie
That the future years had come,
Dancing to a frenzied drum,
Out of the murderous innocence of the sea.

May she be granted beauty and yet not
Beauty to make a stranger's eye distraught,
Or hers before a looking-glass, for such,
20 Being made beautiful overmuch,
Consider beauty a sufficient end,
Lose natural kindness and maybe
The heart-revealing intimacy
That chooses right, and never find a friend.

Helen being chosen found life flat and dull
And later had much trouble from a fool,
While that great Queen, that rose out of the spray,
Being fatherless could have her way
Yet chose a bandy-leggèd smith for man.
30 It's certain that fine women eat
A crazy salad with their meat
Whereby the Horn of Plenty is undone.

In courtesy I'd have her chiefly learned;
Hearts are not had as a gift but hearts are earned
By those that are not entirely beautiful;
Yet many, that have played the fool
For beauty's very self, has charm made wise,
And many a poor man that has roved,
Loved and thought himself beloved,
40 From a glad kindness cannot take his eyes.

May she become a flourishing hidden tree
That all her thoughts may like the linnet be,
And have no business but dispensing round
Their magnanimities of sound,
Nor but in merriment begin a chase,
Nor but in merriment a quarrel.
O may she live like some green laurel
Rooted in one dear perpetual place.

My mind, because the minds that I have loved,
50 The sort of beauty that I have approved,
Prosper but little, has dried up of late,
Yet knows that to be choked with hate
May well be of all evil chances chief.
If there's no hatred in a mind
Assault and battery of the wind
Can never tear the linnet from the leaf.

An intellectual hatred is the worst,
So let her think opinions are accursed.
Have I not seen the loveliest woman born
60 Out of the mouth of Plenty's horn,
Because of her opinionated mind
Barter that horn and every good
By quiet natures understood
For an old bellows full of angry wind?

Considering that, all hatred driven hence,
The soul recovers radical innocence
And learns at last that it is self-delighting,
Self-appeasing, self-affrighting,
And that its own sweet will is Heaven's will;
70 She can, though every face should scowl
And every windy quarter howl
Or every bellows burst, be happy still.

And may her bridegroom bring her to a house
Where all's accustomed, ceremonious;
For arrogance and hatred are the wares
Peddled in the thoroughfares.
How but in custom and in ceremony
Are innocence and beauty born?
Ceremony's a name for the rich horn,
80 And custom for the spreading laurel tree.

June 1919

from *The Tower*

Sailing to Byzantium

I

That is no country for old men. The young
In one another's arms, birds in the trees
—Those dying generations – at their song,
The salmon-falls, the mackerel-crowded seas,
Fish, flesh, or fowl, commend all summer long
Whatever is begotten, born, and dies.
Caught in that sensual music all neglect
Monuments of unageing intellect.

II

An aged man is but a paltry thing,
10   A tattered coat upon a stick, unless
Soul clap its hands and sing, and louder sing
For every tatter in its mortal dress,
Nor is there singing school but studying
Monuments of its own magnificence;
And therefore I have sailed the seas and come
To the holy city of Byzantium.

III

O sages standing in God's holy fire
As in the gold mosaic of a wall,
Come from the holy fire, perne in a gyre,
20   And be the singing-masters of my soul.
Consume my heart away; sick with desire
And fastened to a dying animal
It knows not what it is; and gather me
Into the artifice of eternity.

IV

Once out of nature I shall never take
My bodily form from any natural thing,
But such a form as Grecian goldsmiths make
Of hammered gold and gold enamelling
To keep a drowsy Emperor awake;
30 Or set upon a golden bough to sing
To lords and ladies of Byzantium
Of what is past, or passing, or to come.

1927

Leda and the Swan

A sudden blow: the great wings beating still
Above the staggering girl, her thighs caressed
By the dark webs, her nape caught in his bill,
He holds her helpless breast upon his breast.

How can those terrified vague fingers push
The feathered glory from her loosening thighs?
And how can body, laid in that white rush,
But feel the strange heart beating where it lies?

A shudder in the loins engenders there
10 The broken wall, the burning roof and tower
And Agamemnon dead.
                              Being so caught up,
So mastered by the brute blood of the air,
Did she put on his knowledge with his power
Before the indifferent beak could let her drop?

1923

Among School Children

I

I walk through the long schoolroom questioning;
A kind old nun in a white hood replies;
The children learn to cipher and to sing,
To study reading-books and histories,
To cut and sew, be neat in everything
In the best modern way – the children's eyes
In momentary wonder stare upon
A sixty-year-old smiling public man.

II

I dream of a Ledaean body, bent
10 Above a sinking fire, a tale that she
Told of a harsh reproof, or trivial event
That changed some childish day to tragedy—
Told, and it seemed that our two natures blent
Into a sphere from youthful sympathy,
Or else, to alter Plato's parable,
Into the yolk and white of the one shell.

III

And thinking of that fit of grief or rage
I look upon one child or t'other there
And wonder if she stood so at that age—
20 For even daughters of the swan can share
Something of every paddler's heritage—
And had that colour upon cheek or hair,
And thereupon my heart is driven wild:
She stands before me as a living child.

IV

Her present image floats into the mind—
Did Quattrocento finger fashion it
Hollow of cheek as though it drank the wind
And took a mess of shadows for its meat?

And I though never of Leadaean kind
30 Had pretty plumage once – enough of that,
Better to smile on all that smile, and show
There is a comfortable kind of old scarecrow.

V

What youthful mother, a shape upon her lap
Honey of generation had betrayed,
And that must sleep, shriek, struggle to escape
As recollection or the drug decide,
Would think her son, did she but see that shape
With sixty or more winters on its head,
A compensation for the pang of his birth,
40 Or the uncertainty of his setting forth?

VI

Plato thought nature but a spume that plays
Upon a ghostly paradigm of things;
Solider Aristotle played the taws
Upon the bottom of a king of kings;
World-famous golden-thighed Pythagoras
Fingered upon a fiddle-stick or strings
What a star sang and careless Muses heard:
Old clothes upon old sticks to scare a bird.

VII

Both nuns and mothers worship images,
50 But those the candles light are not as those
That animate a mother's reveries,
But keep a marble or a bronze repose.
And yet they too break hearts – O Presences
That passion, piety or affection knows,
And that all heavenly glory symbolize—
O self-born mockers of man's enterprise;

VIII

Labour is blossoming or dancing where
The body is not bruised to pleasure soul,
Nor beauty born out of its own despair,
60   Nor blear-eyed wisdom out of midnight oil.
O chestnut-tree, great-rooted blossomer,
Are you the leaf, the blossom or the bole?
O body swayed to music, O brightening glance,
How can we know the dancer from the dance?

from *The Winding Stair and Other Poems*

Death

Nor dread nor hope attend
A dying animal;
A man awaits his end
Dreading and hoping all;
Many times he died,
Many times rose again.
A great man in his pride
Confronting murderous men
Casts derision upon
10 Supersession of breath;
He knows death to the bone—
Man has created death.

Coole Park, 1929

I meditate upon a swallow's flight,
Upon an aged woman and her house,
A sycamore and lime-tree lost in night
Although that western cloud is luminous,
Great works constructed there in nature's spite
For scholars and for poets after us,
Thoughts long knitted into a single thought,
A dance-like glory that those walls begot.

There Hyde before he had beaten into prose
10 That noble blade the Muses buckled on,
There one that ruffled in a manly pose
For all his timid heart, there that slow man,

That meditative man, John Synge, and those
Impetuous men, Shawe-Taylor and Hugh Lane,
Found pride established in humility,
A scene well set and excellent company.

They came like swallows and like swallows went,
And yet a woman's powerful character
Could keep a swallow to its first intent;
20 And half a dozen in formation there,
That seemed to whirl upon a compass-point,
Found certainty upon the dreaming air,
The intellectual sweetness of those lines
That cut through time or cross it withershins.

Here, traveller, scholar, poet, take your stand
When all those rooms and passages are gone,
When nettles wave upon a shapeless mound
And saplings root among the broken stone,
And dedicate – eyes bent upon the ground,
30 Back turned upon the brightness of the sun
And all the sensuality of the shade—
A moment's memory to that laurelled head.

Coole Park and Ballylee, 1931

Under my window-ledge the waters race,
Otters below and moor-hens on the top,
Run for a mile undimmed in Heaven's face
Then darkening through 'dark' Raftery's 'cellar' drop,
Run underground, rise in a rocky place
In Coole demesne, and there to finish up
Spread to a lake and drop into a hole.
What's water but the generated soul?

Upon the border of that lake's a wood
10   Now all dry sticks under a wintry sun,
And in a copse of beeches there I stood,
For Nature's pulled her tragic buskin on
And all the rant's a mirror of my mood:
At sudden thunder of the mounting swan
I turned about and looked where branches break
The glittering reaches of the flooded lake.

Another emblem there! That stormy white
But seems a concentration of the sky;
And, like the soul, it sails into the sight
20   And in the morning's gone, no man knows why;
And is so lovely that it sets to right
What knowledge or its lack had set awry,
So arrogantly pure, a child might think
It can be murdered with a spot of ink.

Sound of a stick upon the floor, a sound
From somebody that toils from chair to chair;
Beloved books that famous hands have bound,
Old marble heads, old pictures everywhere;
Great rooms where travelled men and children found
30   Content or joy; a last inheritor
Where none has reigned that lacked a name and fame
Or out of folly into folly came.

A spot whereon the founders lived and died
Seemed once more dear than life; ancestral trees,
Or gardens rich in memory glorified
Marriages, alliances and families
And every bride's ambition satisfied.
Where fashion or mere fantasy decrees
We shift about – all that great glory spent—
40   Like some poor Arab tribesman and his tent.

We were the last romantics – chose for theme
Traditional Sanctity and loveliness;
Whatever's written in what poets name
The book of the people; whatever most can bless
The mind of man or elevate a rhyme;
But all is changed, that high horse riderless,
Though mounted in that saddle Homer rode
Where the swan drifts upon a darkening flood.

Byzantium

The unpurged images of day recede;
The Emperor's drunken soldiery are abed;
Night resonance recedes, night-walkers' song
After great cathedral gong;
A starlit or a moonlit dome disdains
All that man is,
All mere complexities,
The fury and the mire of human veins.

Before me floats an image, man or shade,
10   Shade more than man, more image than a shade;
For Hades' bobbin bound in mummy-cloth
May unwind the winding path;

A mouth that has no moisture and no breath
Breathless mouths may summon;
I hail the superhuman;
I call it death-in-life and life-in-death.

Miracle, bird or golden handiwork,
More miracle than bird or handiwork,
Planted on the star-lit golden bough,
20   Can like the cocks of Hades crow,
Or, by the moon embittered, scorn aloud
In glory of changeless metal
Common bird or petal
And all complexities of mire or blood.

At midnight on the Emperor's pavement flit
Flames that no faggot feeds, nor steel has lit,
Nor storm disturbs, flames begotten of flame,
Where blood-begotten spirits come
And all complexities of fury leave,
30   Dying into a dance,
An agony of trance,
An agony of flame that cannot singe a sleeve.

Astraddle on the dolphin's mire and blood,
Spirit after spirit! The smithies break the flood,
The golden smithies of the Emperor!
Marbles of the dancing floor
Break bitter furies of complexity,
Those images that yet
Fresh images beget,
40   That dolphin-torn, that gong-tormented sea.

1930

from *Parnell's Funeral and Other Poems*

A Prayer for Old Age

God guard me from those thoughts men think
In the mind alone;
He that sings a lasting song
Thinks in a marrow-bone;

From all that makes a wise old man
That can be praised of all;
O what am I that I should not seem
For the song's sake a fool?

I pray – for fashion's word is out
10 And prayer comes round again –
That I may seem, though I die old,
A foolish, passionate man.

Lapis Lazuli

(For Harry Clifton)

I have heard that hysterical women say
They are sick of the palette and fiddle-bow,
Of poets that are always gay, ·
For everybody knows or else should know
That if nothing drastic is done
Aeroplane and Zeppelin will come out,
Pitch like King Billy bomb-balls in
Until the town lie beaten flat.

All perform their tragic play,
10 There struts Hamlet, there is Lear,
That's Ophelia, that Cordelia;
Yet they, should the last scene be there,
The great stage curtain about to drop,
If worthy their prominent part in the play,
Do not break up their lines to weep.
They know that Hamlet and Lear are gay;
Gaiety transfiguring all that dread.
All men have aimed at, found and lost;
Black out; Heaven blazing into the head:
20 Tragedy wrought to its uttermost.
Though Hamlet rambles and Lear rages,
And all the drop-scenes drop at once
Upon a hundred thousand stages,
It cannot grow by an inch or an ounce.

On their own feet they came, or on shipboard,
Camel-back, horse-back, ass-back, mule-back,
Old civilizations put to the sword.
Then they and their wisdom went to rack:

No handiwork of Callimachus,
30 Who handled marble as if it were bronze,
Made draperies that seemed to rise
When sea-wind swept the corner, stands;
His long lamp-chimney shaped like the stem
Of a slender palm, stood but a day;
All things fall and are built again,
And those that build them again are gay.

Two Chinamen, behind them a third,
Are carved in lapis lazuli,
Over them flies a long-legged bird,
40 A symbol of longevity;
The third, doubtless a serving-man,
Carries a musical instrument.

Every discolouration of the stone,
Every accidental crack or dent,
Seems a water-course or an avalanche,
Or lofty slope where it still snows
Though doubtless plum or cherry-branch
Sweetens the little half-way house
Those Chinamen climb towards, and I
50 Delight to imagine them seated there;
There, on the mountain and the sky,
On all the tragic scene they stare.
One asks for mournful melodies;
Accomplished fingers begin to play.
Their eyes mid many wrinkles, their eyes,
Their ancient, glittering eyes, are gay.

An Acre of Grass

Picture and book remain,
An acre of green grass
For air and exercise,
Now strength of body goes;
Midnight, an old house
Where nothing stirs but a mouse.

My temptation is quiet.
Here at life's end
Neither loose imagination,
10   Nor the mill of the mind
Consuming its rag and bone,
Can make the truth known.

Grant me an old man's frenzy,
Myself must I remake
Till I am Timon and Lear
Or that William Blake
Who beat upon the wall
Till Truth obeyed his call;

A mind Michael Angelo knew
20   That can pierce the clouds,
Or inspired by frenzy
Shake the dead in their shrouds;
Forgotten else by mankind,
An old man's eagle mind.

The Spur

You think it horrible that lust and rage
Should dance attention upon my old age;
They were not such a plague when I was young;
What else have I to spur me into song?

The Municipal Gallery Revisited

I

Around me the images of thirty years:
An ambush; pilgrims at the water-side;
Casement upon trial, half hidden by the bars,
Guarded; Griffith staring in hysterical pride;
Kevin O'Higgins' countenance that wears
A gentle questioning look that cannot hide
A soul incapable of remorse or rest;
A revolutionary soldier kneeling to be blessed;

II

An Abbot or Archbishop with an upraised hand
10 Blessing the Tricolour. 'This is not,' I say,
'The dead Ireland of my youth, but an Ireland
The poets have imagined, terrible and gay.'
Before a woman's portrait suddenly I stand,
Beautiful and gentle in her Venetian way.
I met her all but fifty years ago
For twenty minutes in some studio.

III

Heart-smitten with emotion I sink down,
My heart recovering with covered eyes;
Wherever I had looked I had looked upon
20 My permanent or impermanent images:
Augusta Gregory's son; her sister's son,
Hugh Lane, 'onlie begetter' of all these;
Hazel Lavery living and dying, that tale
As though some ballad-singer had sung it all;

IV

Mancini's portrait of Augusta Gregory,
'Greatest since Rembrandt,' according to John Synge;
A great ebullient portrait certainly;
But where is the brush that could show anything

Of all that pride and that humility?
30 And I am in despair that time may bring
Approved patterns of women or of men
But not that selfsame excellence again.

V

My medieval knees lack health until they bend,
But in that woman, in that household where
Honour had lived so long, all lacking found.
Childless I thought, 'My children may find here
Deep-rooted things,' but never foresaw its end,
And now that end has come I have not wept;
No fox can foul the lair the badger swept—

VI

40 (An image out of Spenser and the common tongue).
John Synge, I and Augusta Gregory, thought
All that we did, all that we said or sang
Must come from contact with the soil, from that
Contact everything Antaeus-like grew strong.
We three alone in modern times had brought
Everything down to that sole test again,
Dream of the noble and the beggar-man.

VII

And here's John Synge himself, that rooted man,
'Forgetting human words,' a grave deep face.
50 You that would judge me, do not judge alone
This book or that, come to this hallowed place
Where my friends' portraits hang and look thereon;
Ireland's history in their lineaments trace;
Think where man's glory most begins and ends,
And say my glory was I had such friends.

from *Last Poems*

Long-Legged Fly

That civilization may not sink,
Its great battle lost,
Quiet the dog, tether the pony
To a distant post;
Our master Caesar is in the tent
Where the maps are spread,
His eyes fixed upon nothing,
A hand under his head.
Like a long-legged fly upon the stream
10 *His mind moves upon silence.*

That the topless towers be burnt
And men recall that face,
Move most gently if move you must
In this lonely place.
She thinks, part woman, three parts a child,
That nobody looks; her feet
Practise a tinker shuffle
Picked up on a street.
Like a long-legged fly upon the stream
20 *Her mind moves upon silence.*

That girls at puberty may find
The first Adam in their thought,
Shut the door of the Pope's chapel,
Keep those children out.
There on that scaffolding reclines
Michael Angelo.
With no more sound than the mice make
His hand moves to and fro.
Like a long-legged fly upon the stream
30 *His mind moves upon silence.*

The Circus Animals' Desertion

I

I sought a theme and sought for it in vain,
I sought it daily for six weeks or so.
Maybe at last, being but a broken man,
I must be satisfied with my heart, although
Winter and summer till old age began
My circus animals were all on show,
Those stilted boys, that burnished chariot,
Lion and woman and the Lord knows what.

II

What can I but enumerate old themes?
10 First that sea-rider Oisin led by the nose
Through three enchanted islands, allegorical dreams,
Vain gaiety, vain battle, vain repose,
Themes of the embittered heart, or so it seems,
That might adorn old songs or courtly shows;
But what cared I that set him on to ride,
I, starved for the bosom of his faery bride?

And then a counter-truth filled out its play,
The Countess Cathleen was the name I gave it;
She, pity-crazed, had given her soul away,
20 But masterful Heaven had intervened to save it.
I thought my dear must her own soul destroy,
So did fanaticism and hate enslave it,
And this brought forth a dream and soon enough
This dream itself had all my thought and love.

And when the Fool and Blind Man stole the bread
Cuchulain fought the ungovernable sea;
Heart-mysteries there, and yet when all is said
It was the dream itself enchanted me:

Character isolated by a deed
30 To engross the present and dominate memory.
Players and painted stage took all my love,
And not those things that they were emblems of.

III

Those masterful images because complete
Grew in pure mind, but out of what began?
A mound of refuse or the sweepings of a street,
Old kettles, old bottles, and a broken can,
Old iron, old bones, old rags, that raving slut
Who keeps the till. Now that my ladder's gone,
I must lie down where all the ladders start,
40 In the foul rag-and-bone shop of the heart.

Politics

*'In our time the destiny of man presents its meaning
in political terms.'* – Thomas Mann

How can I, that girl standing there,
My attention fix
On Roman or on Russian
Or on Spanish politics?
Yet here's a travelled man that knows
What he talks about,
And there's a politician
That has read and thought,
And maybe what they say is true
10 Of war and war's alarms,
But O that I were young again
And held her in my arms!

Under Ben Bulben

I

Swear by what the sages spoke
Round the Mareotic Lake
That the Witch of Atlas knew,
Spoke and set the cocks a-crow.

Swear by those horsemen, by those women
Complexion and form prove superhuman,
That pale, long-visaged company
That air in immortality

Completeness of their passions won;
10 Now they ride the wintry dawn
Where Ben Bulben sets the scene.

Here's the gist of what they mean.

II

Many times man lives and dies
Between his two eternities,
That of race and that of soul,
And ancient Ireland knew it all.
Whether man die in his bed
Or the rifle knocks him dead,
A brief parting from those dear
20 Is the worst man has to fear.
Though grave-diggers' toil is long,
Sharp their spades, their muscles strong,
They but thrust their buried men
Back in the human mind again.

III

You that Mitchel's prayer have heard,
'Send war in our time, O Lord!'
Know that when all words are said

And a man is fighting mad,
Something drops from eyes long blind,
30   He completes his partial mind,
For an instant stands at ease,
Laughs aloud, his heart at peace.
Even the wisest man grows tense
With some sort of violence
Before he can accomplish fate,
Know his work or choose his mate.

IV

Poet and sculptor, do the work,
Nor let the modish painter shirk
What his great forefathers did,
40   Bring the soul of man to God,
Make him fill the cradles right.

Measurement began our might:
Forms a stark Egyptian thought,
Forms that gentler Phidias wrought.
Michael Angelo left a proof
On the Sistine Chapel roof,
Where but half-awakened Adam
Can disturb globe-trotting Madam
Till her bowels are in heat,
50   Proof that there's a purpose set
Before the secret working mind:
Profane perfection of mankind.

Quattrocento put in paint
On backgrounds for a God or Saint
Gardens where a soul's at ease;
Where everything that meets the eye,
Flowers and grass and cloudless sky,
Resemble forms that are or seem

When sleepers wake and yet still dream,
60   And when it's vanished still declare,
With only bed and bedstead there,
That heavens had opened.
                              Gyres run on;
When that greater dream had gone
Calvert and Wilson, Blake and Claude,
Prepared a rest for the people of God,
Palmer's phrase, but after that
Confusion fell upon our thought.

V

Irish poets, learn your trade,
70   Sing whatever is well made,
Scorn the sort now growing up
All out of shape from toe to top,
Their unremembering hearts and heads
Base-born products of base beds.
Sing the peasantry, and then
Hard-riding country gentlemen,
The holiness of monks, and after
Porter-drinkers' randy laughter;
Sing the lords and ladies gay
80   That were beaten into the clay
Through seven heroic centuries;
Cast your mind on other days
That we in coming days may be
Still the indomitable Irishry.

VI

Under bare Ben Bulben's head
In Drumcliff churchyard Yeats is laid.
An ancestor was rector there
Long years ago, a church stands near,
By the road an ancient cross.

90   No marble, no conventional phrase;
     On limestone quarried near the spot
     By his command these words are cut:
              Cast a cold eye
              On life, on death.
              Horseman, pass by!

                              September 4, 1938

Notes

from *Crossways*

Down by the Salley Gardens

Yeats said that this very early poem attempted to fill out some lines he remembered an old peasant woman singing. He was pleased when it entered popular culture and was treated as an authentic folk-song. Should readers look for anything in it other than its lyrical simplicity? For instance, the repeated advice to *take love* and *life* (3, 7) *easy* could be read as a hint about how Yeats wanted his verse to sound.

    1 **salley** willow.

from *The Rose*

The Lake Isle of Innisfree

This poem opens with apparent purposefulness – *I will arise and go now* (1), yet it closes not, as the reader might expect, with the poet leaving but with his hearing *lake water lapping with low sounds… in the deep heart's core* (10–12). This raises a question that can be asked at several points in the poem: is the poet chiefly concerned with decision and action or with living in a world of his own imagining? For instance, the mention of something as practical and down to earth as *nine bean-rows* (3) suggests that the isle is a solidly real place, but the exotic landscape of the second stanza looks more like an imagined earthly paradise. To know that in Lough Gill, County Sligo, there is an island called *Innisfree* does not help to clear up the issue of whether in the poem the isle is a real place or an image *in the deep heart's core* (12).

    1 **and go now, and go** does the repetition of *go* strengthen or weaken the poet's decision to travel?

5–7 See Approaches p.107.
   7 **purple** since the name *Innisfree* means 'heather island', Yeats may be implying that the *purple glow* is the heather gleaming in the noon-day sun.
11 Does the sudden appearance of urban imagery set up a successful contrast between the romantic island and the drab city, or does the deliberately 'poetic' word order – *pavements grey* instead of grey pavements – make the city as romantic as the island? See Approaches p.104.

When You Are Old

The stance of the lover-poet here is a traditional one; he reproaches the beloved for her neglect of him and imagines a bleak future in which she will have lost her beauty. The poem, however, does not entirely blame the beloved, because at the close it is *Love* itself that has *fled* (10). In the light of this, the poet's attitude becomes a difficult issue; there is a reproachful edge to the opening (the *ands* drive home just how decrepit and lonely she is) but at the close he apparently draws near and, perhaps, shares her murmuring sadness. The poem was written for Maud Gonne. (See Chronology p.135.)

   2 **this book** a reflexive note; the poet calls attention to the fact that this is the poem she will read when she is *old and grey* (1).

from *The Wind Among the Reeds*

He Wishes for the Cloths of Heaven

This poem has features in common with traditional love poetry; not only is the tone hushed and the poet almost breathless in his adoration but the pattern of thought is familiar: the poet eloquently declares that were he able he would do impossibly lavish things for his beloved but since he is poor he settles for something less extravagant. You may wonder whether the poetry remains emotionally intense or whether, as his romantic imaginings fade, the ardour of his loving cools.

1 **heavens' embroidered cloths** the innumerable stars in the night sky. Might Yeats also be drawing attention to the embroidered quality of his poetry. See *A Coat* (p.12).

7 An echo, perhaps, of Sir Walter Raleigh, who chivalrously spread his cloak at the feet of Queen Elizabeth I.

from *In the Seven Woods*

Adam's Curse

In The Bible (*Genesis* 3) the story of how Adam and Eve were excluded from the Garden of Eden (*Adam's fall*, 22) ends with curses. Adam's curse is that he will live a life of frustratingly hard and unfulfilling work. This poem marks a change in Yeats' style from self-conscious poetic flourishes to a conversational plainness; for instance, the casual *maybe* (4) and the colloquial *marrow-bones* (7). Because it is a conversation poem (a work of informal tone, dealing with personal thoughts and feelings), it is important to follow the drift of the talk and be aware of how the topics emerge.

1 **We sat together** the poem is almost certainly autobiographical in origin: Maud Gonne records an occasion when she (the *you* of the poem), her sister, Kathleen Pilcher – *that beautiful mild woman* (2, 15) – and Yeats talked about beauty, love, marriage and poetry.

4–6 Does the poem live up to the picture of poetry put forward in these lines? See Approaches p.129.

6 **stitching and unstitching** for a similar image see *A Coat* (p.12).

7 **marrow-bones** knees.

9 **pauper** a poor person.

14 **martyrs** those who suffer and die for a cause. What kind of cause?

24 **high courtesy** not just good manners but of love and courtship as a ritualized art. See also *the old high way of love* (36) and Approaches pp.115–6.

27 **idle trade** the contrast here is the familiar one in Yeats between the dignity of a cultured past and a dull and ordinary present.

31 **moon** ˍ the *moon* is clearly important in the poem because at its appearance, conversation ceases. It could be a symbol of the passage of time.

from *The Green Helmet and Other Poems*

No Second Troy

In this poem the poet recognizes that although his is an unheroic age there is, nevertheless, one woman who is marked out by her *nobleness* (7) and *beauty* (8) as being of heroic and even mythical stature. Yeats builds up to the momentous identification of the subject of the poem with Helen of Troy, and, as is often the case, this is achieved through the rhythmical grandeur of the poet's voice. You might think about the implication for the poet: if the woman is Helen, does Yeats become an epic poet in the tradition of Homer – the Greek poet who, in *The Iliad*, wrote of how Helen was the cause of the Trojan War? See Approaches pp.119–20 for Yeats' treatment of Helen and pp.116–7 for a general discussion of the poem.

1 **blame** does the poem refrain from laying *blame* on the woman? *Misery* (2) is a very strong word, but the praise of *high and solitary and most stern* (10) might indicate that the poem has outgrown hurt, resentment and self-pity.
3 **most violent ways** a biographical reading would stress that in her efforts to free Ireland from British rule, Maud Gonne associated with groups, that planned bombings.
7 **simple** an important value word in Yeats' poetry. See *In Memory of Major Robert Gregory* (p.14).

The Mask

This dialogue poem has the charm and elusiveness of a conversation at a masked ball; the one who speaks first wants to know what lies behind the alluring mask, but the wearer resists on the grounds that what matter are the feelings that have been generated, not the real self than is concealed. But, in fact, the poem is even more teasing than that. What it lightly plays with is the question of knowledge. Can the questioner ever know what the wearer is like? The implication is that what lies behind is different (if not, why the reluctance to remove it?) but can we say exactly how the concealed self differs from the mask: neither the questioner nor the reader can know whether the wearer is *deceitful* (7) or an *enemy* (11). It may be that what the poem turns on is the reliability of words themselves; and that, of course, includes the words of this poem.

Yeats himself formulated complex theories about the idea of the mask. To him it was a specially formed public face and an anti-self, a front that was opposite to what persons were really like in their inner selves. The most precise expression of his thought is found in a work called *Autobiographies: What I have called 'The Mask' is an emotional antithesis to all that comes out of their internal nature*. Is this of any help in understanding the poem? See Approaches pp.123–4.

   3 **my dear**   can you be sure of the tone? Is it sinister, sincere or impossible to say?

from *Responsibilities*

'Pardon, Old Fathers'

In this poem Yeats addresses his ancestors and in so doing creates his own image of Ireland – a land of decent, solid men with an engaging variety of gifts who, when there is a need, can be resolute and heroic in action. In the presence of these men, he offers an apology, that because of *a barren passion* (19) – his love for Maud Gonne – he has *no child* (21) to prove himself their descendant. In spite of the repeated *Pardon* (1, 19), you may ask whether the tone is apologetic; pride in his forefathers might be said to be the dominant mood. It is also questionable whether his one achievement – *a book* (21) – is, in spite of the neat, framing negative phrases – *nothing but... Nothing but* (21–2) – the fruit of another kind of passion that has been far from barren. The poem (originally called *Introductory Rhymes*) opened the collection, *Responsibilities*, which Yeats published in 1914. See Approaches p.112.

2 **story's end** the self-presentation of the poet as an old man is increasingly dominant in Yeats' later work.

3 **old Dublin merchant** Yeats thinks that his great-great-grandfather, Benjamin Yeats, was one of the privileged traders who were exempt from ten per cent (wine and tobacco) and four per cent (other goods) import duties.

5–8 Yeats' grandfather, John Yeats, Rector of Drumcliff in County Sligo, knew *Robert Emmet*, who led the unsuccessful 1803 rebellion against the English. John Yeats was known for his kindness to the poor. (See *Under Ben Bulben* p.49 lines 85–6 and *September 1913* p.10 line 21.)

8 **huckster's loin** is this dismissive rejection of the *huckster* – a trader who makes his money through shady dealing – understandably honest pride or snobbish arrogance?

10 Yeats' ancestors married into the *Butler* and *Armstrong* families.

11–12 Here the poet presents his ancestors as fighting for the Protestant William of Orange (*the Dutchman*) against the Catholic James II at the Battle of the Boyne in 1690. The defeat of James left Ireland, a largely Catholic country, under Protestant government.

13 **Old merchant skipper** William Middleton, Yeats' maternal great-grandfather, was a brave and even reckless man who traded between Sligo and Spain.

15 **silent and fierce old man** William Pollexfen, Yeats' maternal grandfather, was a sea captain and trader who said very little and impressed the young Yeats with a sense of his potential anger.

September 1913

The target of this poem is the newer Ireland (largely Catholic, middle-class and commercial), which is characterized as born *to pray and save* (6). Consequently, the poet laments a lost, heroic past while soberly recognizing that a new and narrower world has replaced it. The combination of lament and recognition is particularly felt in the third stanza, where although the old names ring out with mythic force, the poet records that they were failures who succumbed to a *delirium* (22) and are, in the blunt words of the refrain, *dead and gone*. See Approaches pp.111.

1 **you** the money-minded Catholic commercial classes.

1–8 If this refrain has a hint of lyricism and romance about it, the implication may be that in Yeats' poetry *Romantic Ireland* is not yet *dead and gone.*

7 **Romantic Ireland** are the associations of *Romantic* positive – bold, adventurous, heroic, imaginative – or negative – dreamy, impractical, foolish, self-deluding? (Yeats' original title was *Romance in Ireland.*)

8 **O'Leary** John *O'Leary* was an Irish nationalist who, because of his political activities, was imprisoned and exiled over a period of twenty years. In Yeats' view he was a man of broad interests, who saw politics against the rich background of Irish culture. After his death in 1907, Yeats felt that Irish nationalism became narrow and philistine.

11 **wind** contrary associations may be present in this image: are the *names* (10) elemental, adventurous, and invigorating or aimless, destructive, and unpredictable?

17–24 See Approaches p.131.

17 **wild geese** Irishmen who went abroad, mostly to France, Spain and Austria, to serve in the army. They did this because the Penal Laws disadvantaged the Catholic majority.

20 **Edward Fitzgerald** Lord *Edward Fitzgerald* (1763–98) was ejected from the army for proposing a Republican toast in 1792. He died of wounds resisting arrest.

21 **Robert Emmet** *Robert Emmet* (1778–1803) was the leader of an attack upon Dublin Castle, which resulted in the murder of the Lord Chief Justice of Ireland. He was arrested, convicted and at his hanging, drawing, quartering, and beheading refused to have a clergyman present.

Wolfe Tone *Wolfe Tone* (1763–98), although a member of the Church of England, protested against the denial of civil rights to Catholics. Inspired by the American and French Revolutions, he formed the Society of United Irishmen, an organization aimed at achieving political reform and religious equality. He went to France, organized an invasion force, but was arrested by the Royal Navy off the Irish coast. Condemned to death, he committed suicide in prison by cutting his throat.

28–9 Yeats clearly associates the ardour of the Irish Revolutionaries with his love for Maud Gonne. You might think the intrusion of this personal detail inappropriate in a poem about the culture and politics of a nation. A defence would be that it is only in his love that the poet experiences an intense feeling, which can help him understand the commitment of the early nationalists.

The Cold Heaven

This poem may be about a piercingly painful moment of self-understanding, when, prompted by the sudden sight of cold, ice-laden skies, the poet sees the emotional tumults and failures of his past life. At the close he seems to wonder whether the fate of the dead *sent/Out naked on the roads* (10–11), resembles his, facing the skies and recalling his failures.

Such a summary, however, does little justice to the poem's intense emotional drama. Note, for instance, the paradox of ice that burns, the antithesis of youth and age, and the ambiguity of a word such as *riddled* (9), which can mean both shot through (as in riddled by bullets) and puzzled by riddles. These features (and the force of words such as *driven* (3), *wild* (4), *cried and trembled* (8), and *rocked* (8)) enact the emotional turmoil of the poem. It is very difficult to characterize the tone: it could be said to be painful but refreshing and/or devastating yet intoxicating. You may find that the poem continues to provoke questions even when you know it well. It is significant that, like a number of Yeats' poems, it closes with a question. See Approaches p.127.

1 **Suddenly** this word sums up the manner and mood of the poem – the vision of the skies bursts in *suddenly* upon the poet. In connection with the idea that a single word sums up the whole feel of this poem, think about what Peter Ure said:

> **a poem one can never finish describing, and yet which does not need to be described, for it describes itself by what it does.**

6 **love crossed long ago** readers taking a biographical approach will identify this as a reference to Yeats' unsuccessful courtship of Maud Gonne.

8 **trembled** see Approaches p.100.

9–12 Yeats is haunted by an idea that he came across in his reading of occult books, that after death the spirit wanders restlessly, unable to find fulfilment.

9 **quicken** come to life. There is another antithesis here.

12 People sometimes talk about their lives as under the control of the skies. The idea here is that the skies (or the gods) have treated the poet harshly.

The Magi

The story of the Magi – the wise men who travelled to worship the infant Jesus – is found in the second chapter of *St Matthew's Gospel*. It is frequently the subject of paintings, a fact which may account for this poem's pictorial quality. The poem can be read as a re-mythologizing of a familiar story; that is to say, Yeats takes a familiar story and rewrites it to give it a different meaning. If a myth is the imaginative expression, usually in the form of a story, of beliefs that are deeply significant for those who hold them, then the birth of Christ can be read as the myth of God's love and his desire to save humanity. In the myth the wise men stand for those who search for a truth that will save and satisfy. Yeats accepts the outline of the story – the wise men coming to the stable where Christ was born – but re-imagines it in such a way as to change its meaning. Just how radical Yeats' re-mythologizing is, can be seen in his phrase *the pale unsatisfied ones* (2): should not those who have seen Christ be restored to life (and therefore not be *pale*), and should not the encounter be satisfying? The second time *unsatisfied* is used (7), the Magi are still left seeking. See Approaches pp.132–3.

5 **helms** helmets.

7 **Calvary** the hill outside Jerusalem on which Christ was crucified. The word is used here of the crucifixion itself.

8 **uncontrollable mystery** the idea might be that Calvary does not fulfil the promise seen *on the bestial floor*, or that because the *mystery* is *uncontrollable* it never can satisfy. If the last idea is correct, then those who seek will always remain unfulfilled.

A Coat

This is a reflexive poem; that is to say, it is about itself. Its subject matter is Yeats' own poetic practice – the kind of poetry he wrote, and how its language changed. A poem of self-scrutiny might be expected to be earnest, ponderous and even agonized, but, to adopt a metaphor from the poem, its stride is proud and confident and its close is an attractively jaunty swagger. Such an open declaration of poetic ambition is bound to raise questions as to whether Yeats' verse lived up to his ideal: did he discard the *song* (1) of his earlier years? Is it true that he did without *mythologies* (3) or was it only *old* (3) ones that he abandoned? Is there anything in the later poems that corresponds to *walking naked* (10)? See Approaches p.120.

1 **coat** the idea that poetry is like clothing is traditional; they can both be used for show or protection. See *Adam's Curse* p.5 line 6.

3 **mythologies** these are usually identified in criticism as Celtic or, more particularly, Irish legends. Might the myths of Greece and Rome, particularly those about the Trojan War, also be included?

from *The Wild Swans at Coole*

The Wild Swans at Coole

Coole Park in County Galway was the home of Lady Gregory. Yeats, who had first visited it when he was 32, was 51 when he wrote this reflective poem. It can be read as a landscape poem in the tradition of Wordsworth's *Tintern Abbey*, a poem in which the landscape is used as an occasion for the poet to think about the changes in his life. In such a reading the present tenses and the detailed quality of the writing (some of the nouns are qualified by two adjectives) create a solemn, and even majestic, *autumn beauty* (1), which prompts the poet's poignant acknowledgements of the losses and changes in his life. Yet some features of the poem awaken the possibility of other readings. For instance, the thrust of *the water/Mirrors a still sky* (3–4) might be read religiously with its suggestion in *Mirrors* of an unspoilt reflection of a heavenly realm. The *great broken rings* (11) of the swan's flight might be symbolic of the poet's disappointment in love, of an art patterned yet flawed, of Ireland's cultural state or the political turmoils of the age. Similarly, *All's changed* (15) might be read autobiographically, artistically, culturally or politically. You may be unwilling to pursue symbolic readings because the poem is without the deliberate striving after meaning which is often the characteristic of symbolic writing. Yet this may be the poem's real achievement: it allows other than literal readings but does so with ease; like the water, the words are *brimming* (5) with significances, yet those significances are so subdued and controlled that they do not disturb the *still* (4) surface of the language.

12 **clamorous** is the sound at odds with the stillness of the poem? It could be that the poet was *clamorous* in the past but now, in his disappointment, is as quiet as the scene.
14 **sore** you might feel that the poem is serene rather than pained.
25–30 Originally the third stanza was the final one of the poem. Does the rearrangement make a difference?

In Memory of Major Robert Gregory

Robert Gregory was Lady Gregory's only child. He was a skilful landscape painter and he enouraged Yeats to buy the tower – *our house* (1) – at Ballylee. Always a man of action (he was an expert horseman), he enlisted in the Royal Flying Corps (the original name for the Royal Air Force) and before his death on the Italian Front in January 1918 had come to be regarded as an accomplished and daring pilot.

The tone of this tribute to a friend who was both artist and man of action – *Soldier, scholar, horseman* (70, 78, 86) – is dignified and warmly generous. Perhaps one of its achievements is the expression of an emotion that, because it is controlled, never distorts the measured eloquence of the poem and, because it is personal, prevents it from becoming stiffly formal. The development of the poem is also natural: the poet moves easily from recollections of dead friends to thoughts about Gregory and then abruptly closes with what is the equivalent to a choke or the gulping back of tears. The search for the complete life is a preoccupation of Yeats' poetry. See also *An Irish Airman Foresees His Death* (p.18) and Approaches pp.117–8.

1 **house** Yeats used the Norman tower at Ballylee as a summer residence. Its *narrow winding stair* (5) was used by him as a symbol of the ascent of the imagination.

3 **turf** a peat fire.

6 **forgotten truth** given Yeats' interest in the occult, this might refer to ancient wisdom passed on by closed circles of devotees. It could also mean that the people featured in the poem embodied in their lives hitherto concealed aspects of humanity.

8 **all** you might ask yourself why this word is used so frequently in the poem.

9 Yeats is both poet and host in this poem.

17–24 *Lionel Johnson* (1867–1902) was a poet and scholar whom Yeats met in London. He was deeply religious; *brooded upon sanctity* (20) might suggest both the depth and the cost of his devotion. Though introspective he was kind and considerate. *Much falling* (19) might refer to his heavy drinking and/or his keen sense that human life was imperfect and hence fallen. A *measureless consummation* (24) might refer to his preoccupation with life beyond death.

25–32 *John Millington Synge* (1871–1909) was a poet and playwright who was inspired by the people of the west of Ireland who had powerful and sometimes violent feelings but retained a touching and spontaneous innocence. See Approaches p.105.

33–40 *George Pollexfen* (1839–1910) was an uncle of Yeats on his mother's side; a notable horseman in his youth, he later became absorbed in astrology. *Opposition, square and trine* (39) are astrological terms indicating positions of stars. *Sluggish and contemplative* (40) might suggest that he gained spiritual insight at the cost of natural vitality.

34 **Mayo** County Mayo is on the west coast of Ireland, north of County Galway.

47 **Sidney** Sir Philip Sidney (1554–86) is presented here as someone who came close to an ideal of manhood in which learning and action are perfectly blended. Like Robert Gregory, he died in battle.

perfect man we are clearly invited to compare the integrated life of Gregory with the tensions present in the lives of the other friends. Should we also compare Gregory with Yeats?

58–60 *Castle Taylor, Roxborough* (58), *Esserkelly plain* (59) and *Mooneen* (60) are all in County Galway, within about twenty miles of each other.

66 County Clare is south of County Galway.

67–8 Are the artistic qualities of Gregory's work also found in Yeats' poetry?

81–8 The dilemma of the poem emerges here: Yeats presents two alternatives for living – those whose lives are a burning of *damp faggots* (81) will live to have grey hair, but those whose lives are like the burning of *dried straw* (83) will be consumed in an exhilaratingly intense flare, the result of which will be the ugly emptiness of the chimney *gone black out* (84). Can we know which Yeats thinks perferable?

An Irish Airman Foresees His Death

The poem also was prompted by the death of Lady Gregory's son, Robert. It may be significant that Yeats chooses to make the protagonist (the one who speaks in the poem) anonymous. Although the title and subject matter indicate that the poem is set in a war, the airman is metaphorically as well as literally above the politics and communal turmoil. The skies give him a detachment, or freedom, from the war and, in a sense, from his own life. What he becomes absorbed by is the quality of his own mental life and his immediate experiences. How should a reader judge what the airman thinks and feels? In the forceful rhythms and heightened language the reader might feel the presence of a buccaneering spirit. But how should this be judged? Is it a joyful release from a humdrum life into the exhilaration of physical action or the recklessly irresponsible individualism of a man who, because of an absurdly romanticized heroism, has become an emotional mercenary – that is to say, someone who fights not to serve his country but for the sheer thrill of action? See Approaches pp.117–8.

1–2 See Approaches p.104.

1 **fate** by the end of the poem, has this word lost its connotations of grim inevitability and taken on the associations of personal choice and a delight in physical action?

3–4 He fights Germans and guards the English.

5 **Kiltartan** the county north of Robert Gregory's home, Coole Park. The *Cross* may either be crossroads or a wayside cross.

13 **balanced** perhaps the central word of the poem. It may refer

to the airman's struggle to keep his unstable aeroplane in level flight. Alternatively, it may refer to the way the words, phrases and lines of the poem balance and counterbalance each other. A third possibility is that the poem is about the weighing up of options, the options of *this life, this death* (16). By the end you may be left with the question of whether the airman's mind can be said to be *balanced*. See Approaches p.106.

The Living Beauty

The issue of this poem is whether the poet can *draw content* (3) from bronze and marble works of art or whether his is still a *discontented heart* (3), because he longs for a living flesh and blood beauty. He says that he wants to have beauty *cast out of a mould/In bronze* (4–5), but it is not easy to see how committed he is to that: if he really wanted *dazzling marble* (5) would he have called the poem *The Living Beauty*? See Approaches p.127.

  5 **appears** does this suggest the dazzling sight of art or has it implications of the unreal and the illusory? You might also consider the significance of the word's position in the poem.

To a Young Girl

This is not so much a love poem as a poem about what it is to be in love. The poet presents himself as the one who understands, and thereby places his sometime beloved in the role of the one who has forgotten her own feelings. The poem can, therefore, be read as being about the power of art to recreate the past. You may ask yourself whether at the end the emotions are mere memories or are vividly present. The poem was originally addressed to Maud Gonne's daughter, Iseult, but its qualities are not dependent upon the reader knowing this.

  11 **glittered** See Approaches p.108.

The Fisherman

This poem about the poet and his audience raises some troubling questions. Is the poet arrogant in his dismissal of his audience and romantically unrealistic in imagining an ideal one? The arrogance might be present in *commonest ear* (20) and the unrealistic expectation in the idea that the fisherman in Connemara will be a *wise and simple man* (8). A further problem is that if this man *does not exist* (35), to whom is the poet speaking? One possible answer is that the word *audience* (27) is being used in a broad sense to mean any reader who would both understand and approve of what the poet is saying. See Approaches pp.129–30.

4 **Connemara** a remote and mountainous region in the west of County Galway.

13–24 It is probably unwise trying to be biographically specific when interpreting these lines; Yeats is identifying the forces which are antagonistic to any poets.

39–40 How can a poem be both *cold* – hard, clear, impersonal, and *passionate* – ardent, aroused, emotionally committed? You should note that in Yeats, the word *cold* denotes a quality he values. See Approaches pp.126–7.

The People

Although the poem presents itself in biographical terms, its importance is not confined to the relationship between Yeats and Maud Gonne. The honesty that is evident in the admission that he would rather live in Italy clearly derives from tensions in Yeats' life, but the difficulties the poet has with his own culture and the attempt to define the nature of poetic work are features that are important, irrespective of whether there is an actual biographical origin. *The People*'s conversational character recalls *Adam's Curse* (p.5) although unlike that poem, this one arises out of a conversation rather than being about a conversation.

2 **all that I have done** read biographically, this probably means Yeats' poetry, his work for Irish independence and his efforts to establish an Irish theatre.

3 **unmannerly town** Dublin. See Approaches p.111.

4 **served most** a reference to Hugh Lane who tried to build an Art Gallery in Dublin? See *Coole Park, 1929* p.35 line 14.

6–21 This is one of Yeats' most sustained passages about an ideal culture and audience. It should be read in relation to *The*

Fisherman, (p.19) *Coole Park, 1929*, (p.35) and *Coole Park and Ballylee, 1931* (p.37).

9 **Ferrara** the home of Duke Ercole. The Italian writer, Castiglione, whom Yeats admired, related in *The Courtier* how Ercole laid on public plays. Yeats visited *Ferrara* with Lady Gregory and her son, Robert.

11 **unperturbed and courtly images** another instance of praise for art that rises above the turmoil of personal feelings. (See *The Living Beauty* p.18.) Is this poem *courtly* and *unperturbed*?

12–15 Castiglione records in *The Courtier* a story about how the Duchess talked throughout the night on the issue of whether women were capable of divine love.

22–9 After Maud Gonne had separated from her husband, she was hissed during a performance at the Abbey Theatre.

28–9 It looks as if it is her unresentful generosity of spirit that abashed the poet. Is the overcoming of resentment an important issue in Yeats? *Easter 1916* (p.23) and *No Second Troy* (p.7) might be considered in relation to this question.

30 **thought but deed** the tension between a life of thought and one devoted to action is a recurring one in Yeats. *In Memory of Major Robert Gregory* (p.14) is the most sustained exploration of this tension.

32–3 See Approaches p.108.

37 **abashed** made to feel uncomfortable and ashamed.

A Deep-Sworn Vow

Perhaps the best way to appreciate this love poem is to see it as both releasing and subduing emotion. There is considerable pressure behind the repetition of *when* (3, 4, 5), and the climax of the poem is the dramatic *Suddenly* at the opening of the final line. But the syntax of the opening delays the main verb by inserting a reason – her failure to keep the vow – and there is restraint at the close, where it is not revealed whether it is joyful, painful or surprising to meet the beloved's face. It may be that it is this blend of release and restraint that gives the poem a personal and intimate quality, so that readers feel they are intruding upon a private conversation. See Approaches pp.101–2.

2 **friends** this could be an underplayed word for lover or an

indication that because the beloved has failed to keep her vow, the poet has had no deep relationships.

6 **meet** Yeats might have written 'see'. What is gained by using *meet*?

from *Michael Robartes and The Dancer*

Easter 1916

This poem, the title of which is a reminder of *September 1913*, is concerned with the events of the 1916 Easter Rising. On the Easter Monday of that year (24 April), Patrick Pearse, at the head of a volunteer army, occupied the Dublin Post Office and a number of other buildings of strategic significance. From the Post Office, Pearse proclaimed the Irish Free Republic. The British Government sent in troops, and, on the following Saturday, Pearse surrendered. The Rising had little support from Irish people, until the British began executing the leaders. News of their deaths transformed them in people's minds from foolish activists who were distracting Ireland from the War, into martyrs in the cause of liberty.

Yeats is ambivalent, not only in his attitude to the Rising but in the meanings he creates in the poem. For instance, alongside the recognition of change (a central theme) and the new status of Ireland, there is the poet's talk about his *song* (35), the theatrical imagery of *motley* (14) and *the casual comedy* (37). The issue, as so often in Yeats, is whether he is interested in events in themselves or merely as metaphors for the work of the poet. Another issue is the appropriateness of the short line: the poem is about the turbulence of the present, the death of the past and the uncertainty of the future, and yet the line has the trim precision of *Eighteenth-century houses* (4). Is it expansive enough for such important subjects? One defence is that it focuses the poet's unflinching duty to do justice to the events and his refusal to take refuge in emotional outbursts. The issue of line is inseparable from that of tone: the poem could be read as grudging admiration, sober reflection, moral uncertainty, nostalgic regret or bracing honesty. See Approaches pp.112–3 for a discussion of Yeats and politics.

1 **them** the leaders of the Rising.

2 **vivid** should this word be connected with the theatrical imagery which is used in the poem to suggest the quality of Irish life before the Rising, or does it suggest that before the attack the leaders were full of *vivid* life?

4 Central Dublin is a largely *Eighteenth-century* city.

6, 8 **polite meaningless words** a contrast to the *song* (35) which the poet offers in celebration of the leaders of the Rising?

12 **club** what are the appropriate associations – intimate companionship or narrow complacency?

14 **motley** the clothes of a clown, player or jester.

16 **terrible beauty** in what ways are the events both *terrible* and beautiful? Change may terrify; but *beauty* is much harder to understand. Perhaps the selfless nobility of the leaders can be said to be beautiful, and there may even be the hint that the poem itself is a beautiful product of the Rising. For *terrible*, see *The Municipal Gallery Revisited* (12).

17 **That woman** Constance Gore-Booth. She took part in the Rising, was sentenced to death but reprieved.

24 **This man** Patrick Pearse, the lawyer, poet, founder of a school and director of the Volunteers, who took the Post Office. He was proclaimed President of the provisional government of the Irish Republic. At his trial he impressed the judges with his courage and conviction. On 3 May he became the first of the leaders to be shot.

26 **This other his helper** Thomas MacDonagh. He was a poet and playwright who had been the first member of staff at Pearse's school. He was director of training for the Volunteers and was executed on the same day as Pearse.

31 **This other man** John MacBride. He had fought against the British in the Boer War. Yeats' antagonism to him was due to the fact that he had married Maud Gonne. He had not known about the Rising but joined the rebels during Easter Week. He was shot on 5 May. You might think about the significance of including him in the *song* (35), in spite of the fact that he is not praised, as the others are, for possessing qualities admired by Yeats.

37 **casual comedy** if the world before the Rising was a *casual comedy*, what does this imply about what it was afterwards? One possible answer is tragedy (*terrible beauty* could be a vivid

summary of the terrors and wonders of great tragedy); on the other hand, the fact that no name is given could signify that no words are adequate to describe it.

41–56 This section shows how ambivalent the poem is about the Rising. The leaders are seen as the *stone* which *trouble(s) the living stream* (44); although they cause change they appear to be unnatural because they themselves do not change. Nevertheless, this section closes with an affirmation of their centrality – *in the midst of all* (56). It might be thought odd that a poem about events in Dublin should contain so much imagery about the countryside. Its presence could either mean that the Rising failed because it lost touch with the traditions of the countryside or that it actually threatened those things. See Approaches p.130.

43 **Enchanted** the implications could be either those of magic and romance or of delusion and distraction.

68 **keep faith** the British Government had promised that they would enact the Bill granting Home Rule to Ireland when the war finished.

70 **dream** does this mean a noble ideal or a hopeless longing?

73 **Bewildered** this could be read positively as admirable dedication or negatively as meaning that they were misguided. The same is true of *excess* in the previous line.

76 **Connolly** James Connolly. He was active in Irish Trades Union work and commanded the Republican forces in the Easter Rising. Because he had been wounded in the foot he was strapped to a chair when he was executed on 12 May.

78 **green** the traditional colour of Ireland.

Sixteen Dead Men

After the Easter Rising (see *Easter 1916* p.23) fourteen men were shot in Dublin, one in Cork, and in London Sir Roger Casement was executed (hanged, not shot) for treason. You might ask if this poem is as ambivalent as *Easter 1916*, or whether the poet is more certain of the significance of those who have died? This question is related to the issue of tone: is it best described as blunt? proud? stirring? defiant? reckless? Another interesting issue is how the ballad or popular song form is used as an expression of the poem's distinctive stance.

1 **But**   only.
5 **loitering**   does this word stress their potential danger, their eerie persistence beyond death, or the odd, and somewhat out of place, suggestion of loutishness?
7–8 One of the Irish objections to the Rising was that it distracted people from the war effort.
10 **Pearse**   see *Easter 1916* (24)
12 For *MacDonagh*, see *Easter 1916* p.23 line 26. The puzzling *bony thumb* might be a defiant gesture.
16 See *September 1913* p.26 lines 20–1. It is interesting that this poem deals with the past, whereas the more sophisticated *Easter 1916* does not.

The Second Coming

Many critics read this famous but difficult poem as an expression of Yeats' belief that history moves in cycles (or gyres) and that a cycle of reason, restraint and tenderness, represented by Christianity with its emphasis on the child in the cradle, is giving way to one dominated by uncontrolled emotions, violence and blood. In support of this interpretation is the fact that Yeats devoted a good deal of energy to formulating an elaborate theory of history which was based upon a series of gyres. He also provided a quite lengthy commentary on the poem, which is largely taken up with mathematical speculations (including a diagram) about the course of future history. He wrote that *the life gyre is sweeping outward* (the opening two lines of the poem?) and that *the revelation which approaches will form a contrary movement.*

But readers need not accept this approach. The poem could be understood as the work of someone who is appalled by the present and anxious about the future and who, in order to express and bring shape to his feelings, produces a medley of images which are impressive, but do not amount to a theory of history. Support for this may be found in the argument that what is impressive about the poem is not a theory of history (is it even there in the poem?) but a sense of foreboding, and the bold way in which the poet attempts to interpret contemporary events. See Approaches p.123.

1–2 Yeats may have chosen the image of the *falcon* circling out of reach, because falconry was part of those refined cultures, that valued *ceremony* (6), and that under pressure from the *anarchy... loosed upon the world* (4), were being destroyed.

The image might suggest that civilization is increasingly out of touch with Christ or, more generally, that there is a breakdown in communications and relationships. See Approaches p.123.

1 **gyre** a spiralling movement that grows ever wider.

3–8 Are these lines better than the ones in the second half of the poem (9–22), or is there a continuity between the two sections that makes it impossible to judge one section better than the other? It might be said that, in comparison with the cloudy musings of the second part, these lines are exact and intellectually taut while exerting a strong emotional pressure. Another argument is that the lines are genuinely universal in that they can be applied to very many situations (they are frequently quoted). Against these points is the view that since the second half bears out the prophetic judgements of the first, there is a consistency as well as a continuity in the poem.

6 **ceremony of innocence** this could be understood as baptism, in which case this line might mean that as the world collapses the ritual of cleansing is itself drowned. Another possibility is that *ceremony* might refer to those things that sustain civilization – ritual, art, manners, custom.

9–11 These lines can be read either as the poet asking questions or as his hearing the cries (anxious and/or expectant?) of people who are fearful about the future.

12 *Spiritus Mundi* literally, the spirit of the world. It may mean a storehouse or collective memory of hauntingly powerful images and myths.

13–17 This figure resembles the Sphinx, a huge ancient Egyptian statue near the Pyramids which has a lion's body and a human head – but is not named as such in the poem. However, the Sphinx is seated, and is not usually thought of as having a *blank and pitiless* gaze (15).

18–22 The close of the poem brings out how different it is from traditional Christian teaching. Christianity teaches that at the end of time Christ will return in glory to judge the world, whereas here there is no finality, only a *rough beast* (21) about to be born. Some critics say the poem should have been called 'The Second Advent' or 'The Second Birth'.

18 **darkness drops** the fact that the word *drops* is associated with the theatre (curtains drop at the end of a performance) might prompt the thought that there is something theatrical, perhaps even stagey, about the vision of the *shape* (14) moving in *the desert* (13).

19 **stony sleep** this could be twenty centuries of Christianity or the sleep of the beast.

20 **rocking cradle** possibly a reference to the birth of Christ.

22 **Bethlehem** Christ was born in Bethlehem.

A Prayer for My Daughter

This poem, written soon after the birth of his daughter, Anne, in 1919, can be read as an exploration of Yeats' belief in the values which sustain civilization; in the words of Harold Bloom, it is *a complete map of Yeats' social mind*. Which words embody those beliefs? *Custom* (80) is clearly one: which are the others? It is also worth asking whether the language of the poem displays the values of civilized courtesy which it celebrates, and if so, how? Asking these questions raises the problem of whether, in spite of the title, the poem's chief subject is the poet. If this is so, what do you make of the daughter? Does she essentially exist as someone whom the poet has imagined? Finally, in what senses is it a prayer; for instance, it makes requests, but to whom are they made? See Approaches pp.125–6 for a discussion of courtesy.

1–3 See Approaches p.100.

1 **storm** is the *storm* in the poet's mind – *excited reverie* (13) – and/or is it the world that is undergoing a cultural and political storm of violent change?

2 **cradle-hood** there are links between this poem and *The Second Coming*: both, for instance, contain the word *cradle* and both mention the sea. When they were first published, *A Prayer For My Daughter* immediately followed *The Second Coming* (p.26). What difference, if any, has the birth of the child made to the poet's understanding of the world?

coverlid a variant of coverlet, the upper covering on a cradle or bed.

4 **Gregory's Wood** the poem is set in the tower which was Yeats' home in the summer months. It was near Coole Park, the

country house of his friend, Lady Gregory. See also line 10.

5 **roof-levelling** the word *levelling* can be used in a political
sense to mean bringing everybody down to the same level. Is it
possible to see what the poet's attitude to this might be? For
more on *wind*, see Approaches p.119.

8 **great gloom** is the *gloom* the poet feels present in the poem?

13 **excited reverie** does this almost paradoxical phrase sum up
the mood of this and others of Yeats' poems?

16 **murderous innocence** when thinking about the meaning of
this phrase, you should bear in mind *radical innocence* (66) and
The Second Coming p.26 lines 4–5

17–32 See Approaches p.108.

25 **Helen** Helen of Troy. See notes on *No Second Troy* (p.7).
The *fool* may be Paris, the Trojan prince who stole Helen from
her husband, Menelaus.

27 **that Great Queen** Venus, or Aphrodite, is the goddess of love
in classical mythology, who was born out of the sea.

29 **bandy-legged smith** Venus took as her husband Vulcan, or
Hephaestus, the lame blacksmith to the classical gods.

32 **the horn of plenty** in classical mythology Jupiter, or Zeus, was
given a *horn* which overflowed with the food of the gods. In
literature it often stands for the richness and abundance of life.

33 **courtesy** it is worth noticing that the qualities this word
stands for – order, discipline and tact – are also qualities associ-
ated with works of art.

48 **one dear perpetual place** of what is this an image? Does it
work solely on the level of nature or does it carry with it
cultural, social or even political implications?

52 **hate** how free from hatred is this and others of Yeats' poems?

56 The *linnet* and *leaf* are images of two things perfectly and natur-
ally united.

58 **opinions** is Yeats drawing a distinction between *opinions* –
mere passing fashions – and the *excited reverie*, with its associa-
tions of passion and contemplation, out of which this poem
emerges? Another approach to this word is through the way in
which Yeats presents men and women: is there the suggestion
that men can hold opinions and remain balanced, whereas
women who try to think are in danger of giving way to shrill
ranting?

59 **the loveliest woman born** usually identified as Maud Gonne.
See Approaches p.115.

66–9 How successful are these crucial lines? The poem has insisted upon order (*courtesy*) but the vivid phrase *self-delighting,/Self-appeasing, self-affrighting* (67–8) points to the need to satisfy not society but the individual. Such self-expression is usually thought of as being at odds with the cultivation of a civilized society. It could be argued that the identification of the individual's will with *Heaven's will* (69) removes the difficulty, but it might be thought that this is too vague to resolve the issue.

66 **radical** Yeats may be requiring the reader to remember that one of the original meanings of this word was 'of, or pertaining to roots'. What implications might this have for the meaning of the poem?

73 **bridegroom** is it possible to glean from the poem what kind of husband Yeats has in mind?

76 **thoroughfares** does this aristocratic disdain for the common people make it difficult for readers to accept Yeats' thinking, or does the poet succeed in making it clear that an aristocracy of some kind is necessary in order to preserve culture?

from *The Tower*

Sailing to Byzantium

This lyrical and passionate poem centres on tensions which lie at the heart of Yeats' poetry; particularly, the frustrations of growing old and the relationship between human life, which is subject to time, and the *Monuments* (8) of art, which are beyond it. The poet wants to move away from the world of *Fish, flesh, or fowl* (5) – the natural world in which time passes – to one in which he is *out of nature* (25) and beyond the attacks of time. Yeats' symbol for this world is Byzantium (the modern Istanbul), which, until its capture by the Turks in 1453, was a highly sophisticated city, celebrated for beauty in the visual arts and the drama and mystery of its elaborate religious ritual.

But does the poem work by praising art at the expense of life? Is there, for instance, any real difference between the world he wants to move away from, the world of *Whatever is begotten, born, and dies*

(6) and the state he finds desirable at the close of the poem, when, in the Emperors' Palace, he listens to the mechanical bird singing *Of what is past, or passing, or to come* (32)? The poem is intriguingly and teasingly full of such problems. See Approaches pp.124–5.

1 **country** this word's use might indicate that Yeats had a particular country in mind (Ireland?), but the talk about time passing could be read to mean that he is thinking of the human condition of living in time.

3 Are both *the young* (1) and the *birds* (2) the *dying generations*, and are they both *at their song*? In the case of *the young, their song* could be either what they sing or, on a symbolic level, the passion expressed in their love.

4 Do you feel the agony of the falling salmon and the sickly profusion of the seas, or do the words vividly suggest the vigour and the plenty of nature?

5 **all summer long** you might think that this is enough to content people and is, in any case, warmer, more immediate and more attractive than the passionless *Monuments of unageing intellect* (8) that the poet is apparently praising.

7 **Caught** an ambiguous word: does it mean fascinated and enraptured, or deluded and deceived?
music the word looks as if it refers to the pulsating rhythms of life but it might also point to the rhythms of the poem itself. Do those rhythms *commend* (5) the life people and animals live?

8 **Monuments of unageing intellect** the cold and formal associations of *Monuments* and the rational quality of *intellect* might be taken as summing up the impersonal quality of art which is beyond time. If you feel the magnificence of the *Monuments*, then you might agree with the poet in finding them more wonderful than the works of nature. See Approaches p.121.

9–10 See *Among School Children* p.32 line 32.

11 Does the poet show us that the singing of the *soul* is different from the singing of the birds or the young? If the line is about art (poetry is often spoken of as song), there is the teasing problem that a great deal of song is about what the poet says he wants to move away from – the world of nature and the young in love.

13 **studying** the thoughtful appreciation of art. Is the poem concerned with studying or with the making of art?

15 The poem is called *Sailing to Byzantium*, but here the poet claims he has arrived. Given the tensions in the poem, you might ask: has he?

17 **sages** the wise who here stand for those who create or help others to understand the *Monuments* (8) of the soul's magnificence.

19 **perne** move in a circular or spiralling movement. It looks as if Yeats is asking the *sages* (17) to enter once more the world of ordinary flesh and blood, so he can be guided through it to their happy state beyond it.

21 **consume** to burn away or purge. The idea that in order to be fit for eternal life the soul must have all that is unworthy in it burnt away is one that appears in many religious traditions.

24 **artifice** that which has been made. Although the poem increasingly praises what has been made rather than what is natural, it might be felt that the word *artifice* brings with it unfortunate associations of artificiality and even falseness.

27–32 The usual explanation of these lines is that Yeats had read about a golden tree with artificial singing birds, that stood in the palace of the Byzantine Emperor. The fact that the word 'bird' is not mentioned might indicate that Yeats is interested in the process of its making and its artistic status rather than its resemblance to a natural form.

Leda and the Swan

In classical mythology Zeus (or Jupiter) took the form of a swan and raped Leda; the child she bore was Helen of Troy. Yeats could be attempting to create the intense experience of a mythical event. The drama of the writing could then be understood as his way of bringing home to the reader why it is that myths haunt the imagination. The poem can also be read as being about art itself, the forceful coming of inspiration, which, in time, creates a work of art. A third possibility is that it is about something more general: the process by which opposites (in this case a god and a human being) violently meet, struggle and produce a new thing. Whatever you make of it, justice should be done to its vivid immediacy (we feel we are witnessing an actual event) and the sense that important symbolic meanings are present. See Approaches pp.120–1.

3 **webs** the folds of skin between the claws of the swan.

/ **white rush** perhaps the best way of understanding this phrase is to realize that the girl would see the swan as a *rush* of whiteness.

8 What do you make of this line? On one level it is warm and intimate (as also is *breast upon his breast* in line 4), but you might be aware of an alien quality in *strange* and be disturbed by the pun in *lies*.

10–11 These fragmentary lines evoke the destruction of Troy and the murder, upon his return home, of the leader of the Greek forces, *Agamemnon*.

12–14 Appropriately, the question with which the poem ends receives no answer. What it does is generate a further question: what *knowledge?* It could be of future events, of art (*mastered*) or the force of myth.

Among School Children

Yeats wrote this poem in 1926 after a visit to a school run by nuns on modern educational lines (6). He was by then a famous man; in 1923 he was awarded the Nobel Prize for Literature and since 1922 he had been a Senator of the Irish Free State, hence *public man* (8). An approach may be made through 51, where the poet speaks of *a mother's reveries*. Reverie, a state of musing, imagining or day-dreaming, aptly sums up the manner of the poem: the poet dreams, remembers, pictures and speculates as he gently and thoughtfully meanders from topic to topic. But does this make the poem loose and drifting? One defence is to concentrate on change or progress within the poem: it moves from real children to images of a single child and then, appropriately, to a meditation on the relationship between natural things and images. Another way of seeing a shape in the poem is to pay attention to the trios: there are *Presences* (53) that are known by *passion, piety or affection* (54); in stanza six there are three classical thinkers; the poem deals with children, the young in love and the old, and the image of the chestnut-tree at the close of the poem is of *leaf, the blossom or the bole* (62).

3 **cipher** to read a code, though here it probably means rational activities, such as mathematics and reading, rather than artistic ones summed up by the word *sing*. Is it possible to see what

Yeats' attitude to this is? Is the all-embracing image of the dance at the close of the poem an indication that he favours learning that is whole, easy and joyful rather than the labour of separate activities such as reading and mathematics?

7–8 See Approaches p.110.

9 **Ledaean** in the manner of, and related to Leda. See *Leda and the Swan* (p.31). A possible link between the two poems is that *Leda and the Swan* deals with the conception of a child, while this one is about the rearing of children. For a reference to Maud Gonne see Approaches pp.114–5.

10–11 The *she* (10) can be read as Maud Gonne, but no name appears in the poem, and the tale is introduced as part of the musing poet's dream.

15–16 *Plato* (41) has a character in one of his philosophical dialogues argue that since people have been divided into men and women, love is a search for a lost unity. In his *Symposium*, Plato compares the division of people into men and women to slicing an egg in two.

21 **paddler** perhaps an echo of Hans Anderson's story of the Ugly Duckling.

24 **living child** one of the strongest tensions in Yeats emerges here. The poem (like many of Yeats') moves away from living things towards the images art creates, yet here (and elsewhere) he is thrilled by the presence of the *living child*. However, the child becomes a living reality only through the art of the poet.

26 **Quattrocento** the art of the Italian Renaissance as it flourished in the Fifteenth century. It is characteristic of Yeats that the fading of natural beauty, which is often compared to the unchanging beauty of art, should be presented in terms of art.

30 **plumage** the image of the swan implied by *Ledaean* (29) becomes a source of other images in the poem. A case of *Those images that yet/Fresh images beget* (*Byzantium* 38–9)?

32 **scarecrow** See *Sailing to Byzantium* p.30 line 10.

34 Scholars point out that Yeats was familiar with the Greek philosopher Porphyry, who speculated that the pleasure of sexual intercourse acted like honey in drawing the unborn soul towards birth. The line might also work by establishing a contrast between the honey of lovemaking that leads to generation and the disappointment and frustrations of life that seem to betray the hopes present in the ecstasy of the sexual act.

36 The idea is that the new-born child will be contented or

restless, depending upon whether there is remembrance or forgetfulness of its happy state before birth.

41–8 See Approaches p.107.

41 **Plato** the fifth-century BC Greek philosopher who taught that the material world was not the ultimate reality but the reflection in space and time of a pure world of forms.
Spume is the froth that gathers on disturbed water.

42 **paradigm** a pattern or ideal form which acts as an exemplifying model of individual things. Plato's world consisted of pure forms that were a set of paradigms for things that only existed imperfectly in the material world. Calling the forms *ghostly* makes them less real than the material world and raises, once again, the question of whether the world of ideas is less attractive than the world of things.

43 **Aristotle** the fourth-century BC Greek philosopher who took man's acquaintance and understanding of the material world as the starting point of his thought. He could, therefore, be said to be *solider* than Plato.

44 *Aristotle* was tutor to Alexander the Great. In accordance with the down-to-earth nature of his philosophy, he is imagined as beating the future *King of Kings* with a leather whip, *the taws*.

45 **Pythagoras** the sixth-century BC Greek philosopher who worked out the mathematical relations in music. The phrase *golden-thighed* is an ancient description which suggests his god-like status; as such it is a grim contrast to the fact that he, like Plato and Aristotle, was reduced by age to *Old clothes upon old sticks* (48).

47 **Muses** in classical mythology the semi-divine inspirers of art and poetry.

49 **worship** having looked at thinkers, the poet now turns to thinking about religious worship. Is it possible to see what his attitude is?

52 Compare this line with the thought of *The Living Beauty* (p.18).

61–4 In order to appreciate the close of the poem, you should attend to the pace, rhythm and pitch of the lines. When thinking about their meaning, it must be remembered that Yeats is using images rather than abstract concepts; nevertheless, the last line is about what we can know and not just what we can see. If the lines seem difficult, you should think about how the inseparability of *leaf, the blossom or the bole* (62) from the *chestnut-tree* (61) acts as a parallel to the inseparability of the elements in a work of art. The context of these lines is the search throughout the poem for a way of living that does justice to the reality of human life. Does the image of the dance work, and if so, can you say why?

62 **bole**   the trunk of a tree.

from *The Winding Stair and Other Poems*

Death

This terse, solemn, and perhaps austere poem has a tone of a serious declaration of belief. It may, therefore, reveal things that are central to Yeats' poetry: the importance of consciousness and awareness, the praise of A *great man* (7), the admiration of heroic defiance and, perhaps the most important of all, the ability of people to shape the meaning of the world through their thought and imagination. The poem was prompted by the assassination, on his way to mass, of Kevin O'Higgins (1892–1927), the Minister of Justice in the Irish Free State. He had been blamed for the tough line taken against independent groups, who used guns; his killers were three ex-members of the IRA.

  1 **attend**   wait for or upon.
  6 **rose**   several meanings are possible here: resurrection, reincarnation (a topic that interested Yeats), or the renewal of courage in the face of constant danger.
 10 **supersession**   the objective and unemotional tone of this word (the superseding – discontinuing – of an act) establishes the mood of the close.
 12 This idea is central to the poem and vital for understanding Yeats as a whole. How is *created* used? Is it wholly metaphoric? For the thought behind this line, see Approaches p.133.

Coole Park, 1929

Coole Park was the home of Lady Gregory, the friend and encourager of Yeats who worked with him in the establishment of the Irish Theatre. The poem is both personal and political. Yeats meditates on his friends – some living, some dead – and celebrates them as artists, who were inspired by the culture of a great house; but it is also about how a small group can, by representing all that is best in Ireland, be the upholders of a high culture. In this respect it can be compared to *The People* (p.20), a poem in which the Court of Urbino, centred round its Duchess, stands, as does Coole Park, for the maintenance of a cultured tradition. See *Coole Park and Ballylee, 1931* (p.37) and Approaches p.117.

  1 **swallow's flight** this phrase may be used for one or several of the following reasons: the birds make light, skimming movements of great artistry; swallows fly in circular and spiralling patterns; they are migratory, and hence visitors and not permanent residents; they are associated with the summer; they sometimes symbolize the soul.

  3 **night** the *night* could mean the poet's approaching death and/or the night of ignorance that comes after the collapse of civilization.

  8 Compare *Among School Children* p.32 lines 63–4.

  9 **Hyde** Douglas Hyde (1860–1949) was a poet and scholar. *Beaten into prose* might mean that he struggled heroically to frame his thoughts or that his poetic gifts faded.

 10 **Muses** see *Among School Children* p.32 line 47.

 11 **one** Yeats?

 13 **John Synge** see *In Memory of Major Robert Gregory* p.14 line 25.

14–24 This section has links with *The Second Coming* (p.26); both are concerned with culture, the threat to *intellectual sweetness* (23) and the place of a centre.

 14 **Shawe-Taylor** John *Shawe-Taylor* (1866–1911), a nephew of Lady Gregory who was handsome, active and impetuously daring.

     Hugh Lane Sir *Hugh Lane* (1875–1915), another nephew of Lady Gregory. He made a very fine collection of Impressionist paintings, which he offered to Dublin on condition that they built an art gallery. Because they refused, the pictures went to London, where they remain. See *The Municipal Gallery Revisited* p.44 line 22.

 24 **time** art is frequently praised for being timeless.

     withershins in a direction opposite to the expected one.

32 **laurelled head** Yeats imagines Lady Gregory crowned with laurel leaves, a sign of artistic eminence.

Coole Park and Ballylee, 1931

Because this poem clearly continues the thought of *Coole Park, 1929*, you may want to ask whether there are any significant differences. Is it, for instance, important that in this poem there are no names? The two chief concerns of the poem are the soul (in the earlier part the poet searches for appropriate emblems for the soul), and the cultural significance of Coole Park. The implication might be that the soul can only thrive in a rich and traditional culture. It is not easy to assess the tone: it could be read as dark and regretful or as defiantly proud.

2 In a poem that seeks for emblems (or symbols), it is interesting to ask whether the *otters* and *moor-hens* are emblematic or just part of the natural scene.

4 Yeats imagined that a swallow hole took water underground from near his tower at Ballylee to Coole Park. He also thought that it was what *Raferty*, the blind ('*dark*') Irish poet (1784–1835), was referring to when he wrote of a '*cellar*' in Ballylee. See Approaches p.112.

6 **demesne** the land belonging to an estate.

8 Does this question arise naturally or does it emerge awkwardly? According to some of the authors Yeats read, in particular Porphyry (see *Among School Children* p.32 lines 33–40), water is the medium through which souls move when they are to be born.

10 **dry sticks** the trees in winter, or an emblem of a lifeless and brittle civilization?

11 **copse** a small group of trees.

12 **tragic buskin** in Athenian tragedy the players wore high boots, or buskins. Consequently, the phrase means 'in the tragic manner'.

17–24 See Approaches p.106.

20 The sudden appearance and disappearance of the swan makes it an apt symbol for the soul passing into and out of life, and thence into the hereafter. Alternatives are that it stands either for a flash of inspiration, or for inspiration leaving the poet.

23–4 The purity and frailty of *knowledge* (22) is like the innocence which is drowned in *The Second Coming* p.20 line 6.

25–6 Lady Gregory who was very infirm in 1931.

30 **last inheritor** Robert Gregory, Lady Gregory's son.

34 Should we compare the *ancestral trees* with the *dry sticks* (10)?

38 These words are best understood in contrast to the celebration of tradition in 27–37.

41–2 A summary of Yeats' themes? Does this poem display the qualities of *Traditional sanctity and loveliness*?

41 **last romantics** Yeats probably meant something wider than poets who flourished in the Romantic period (late eighteenth and early nineteenth centuries) because he closes the stanza with talk of the Greek poet *Homer*.

43–4 *The book of the people* – the popular imagination or things people value – is actually named by poets. This could mean that it is poets who embody the popular imagination, or that poets are cultural leaders who decide, by naming, what the values of the people will be.

46 An echo of *Easter 1916* (p.23)?

high horse Pegasus, the winged horse of Greek mythology, was often used as a symbol of the aspiring imagination of the poet. Note that the horse is said to be *high* – active and energetic – but *riderless* – without direction.

47 **Homer** the blind Greek poet who wrote *The Iliad* and *The Odyssey*. He probably stands here for the first great poet of European culture.

Byzantium

In *Sailing to Byzantium* the poet spoke of what form he would take when he had passed *out of nature* (25). This poem is spoken from the viewpoint of one who has done that, of one who has had his heart consumed (see *Sailing to Byzantium* p.30 line 21) and is beyond *The fury and the mire of human veins* (8). The strangeness of this state (we do not know what it would be like to be without a body) is present in the poem's flickering images which, in the words of the poem, *float(s)* (9), *unwind* (12), *flit* (25), *break* (34, 37) and *beget* (39). This means that the poem cannot be read as a step-by-step argument but might be viewed as a series of vivid and complex pictures. One way of understanding this flow of images is to think of them as passing through the poet's mind as he hears the *great cathedral gong* (4) strike. Another way of appreciating the drift of the poem is to see how its kaleidoscopic movement is similar to abstract art (including collage) and the cinema. (The poem was written in 1930, when those two art forms were very popular.) The poem's 'music' is unmistakeable: its rhythms, cadences, textures and rhymes all work together with a kind of symphonic power. All readings of the poem should try to do justice to the way its meanings are richly and magnificently sounded. See Approaches pp.124–5.

1 **unpurged images** these could be either the *unpurged* (unpurified) *images* of the world (soldiers and prostitutes (2–3)) or the images of the poem itself. If the former, then the poem, like *Sailing to Byzantium*, starts in the world of flesh and blood before moving out of nature. If the latter, the poem can be read as being about the way in which poetic images are purified, refined and clarified. In other words, the poem can be read as being about the writing of poetry. See Approaches p.130.

3–4 You might like to think about how the contrast between the prostitute's voice (*night-walkers' song*) and the sonorous striking of the *great cathedral gong* is acted out in the alliterations and, above all, the rhyme.

5 **moonlit dome** probably the Cathedral of the Holy Wisdom, the great domed church of Byzantium.

7 **mere complexities** can the struggles of living with the tensions and trials (*complexities*) of flesh and blood be so easily dismissed? They have, after all, formed the basis of most literature, including Yeats'.

8 **mire** literally, a bog. You might ask exactly which connotations of the word we should bring to mind.

9–16 This verse raises one of the biggest problems in the poem: it looks as if we are intended to see the image that floats before the poet as above humanity – *superhuman* (15) – but can we overcome the implications of *mummy-cloth* (11) and *breathless* (14), both of which suggest the lifelessness of death? Similarly, the careful distinctions in 10 – *more than... more... than* – suggest that the image is more refined than either *man or shade* (9), but you might think the idea incredible (more than man?) and the resulting image remote and inhuman.

9 **shade**   ghost or spirit.

11 **Hades' bobbin**   *Hades* was the underworld, the realm of the dead. The *bobbin* could be either a spirit who leads the dead down *the winding path* (12) or a spindle which the dead wind as they are led into the underworld. On a symbolic level, it could mean that our earthly lives should be thought of as wound up as a thread is on a spool and that the purging of the self after death is an unwinding.

16 Can *death-in-life* mean the same as *life-in-death*?

17–24 See *Sailing to Byzantium* p.30 lines 27–32.

20 **cocks of Hades**   instead of heralding the dawn and singing in tune with the rhythms of nature, *the cocks of Hades crow* (we don't know what about) and *scorn* (21) *complexities of mire or blood* (24).

22–3 The problem of the poem is whether the *glory of changeless metal* is preferable to *Common bird or petal*.

25 **pavement**   Yeats had read that the spacious area in the centre of Byzantium was called the *pavement*.

26 **flames**   these could be either spirits who have been purged, or the divine flame that purifies *blood-begotten spirits* (28).

29 The act or process of purging.

33–4 Yeats is using an ancient belief that dolphins carry the dead across the sea to the islands of the blessed. The wording is important: by speaking about *the dolphin's mire and blood*, Yeats seems to be finding a place for flesh and blood existence in a poem praising the purified world of spirit and art. *Astraddle* is an ungainly word which enforces the physical dimension of riding on a dolphin's back.

34 **break**   the word *break* is central in the closing stanza; *the flood, bitter furies* (37), *images* (38) and the *sea* (40) are all broken. The violence of the word and the turbulence of the stanza's rhythms enact the struggle to tame and purify the natural energies of life. This stanza may be the most exciting because it confronts and implicitly celebrates what the rest of the poem is trying to deny.

38–40 At least two readings are possible here. The *images* that *beget* new *images* could be those created by a purified art and which show the world of *mire and blood* (33) as torn and tormented. If so, the poem ends with images being purged, a clear contrast to the unpurged ones of the opening line. Another reading sees the images as natural (the turbulent sea is suggestive of wildness, sexuality and fury) and thereby insists that although art breaks them they nevertheless *beget* (a word used of human reproduction) yet more *bitter furies of complexity* (37).

from *Parnell's Funeral and Other Poems*

A Prayer for Old Age

The chief critical issue of this poem is not the interpretation of its subject matter but the question of its success. By rejecting the wisdom of age and choosing the foolish passions associated with youth, the poet runs the risk of forgetting that all art should be controlled and not merely the outpourings of passion. Is the seventh line, O *what am I that I should not seem*, clumsy, or a convincing cry of anguish? The other possible view is that the roughness of the writing is intended to show that the passions that should be absent in old age are still present. See *An Acre of Grass* (p.43), *The Spur* (p.43) and Approaches p.119 and pp. 128–9.

 1 How should this be read? Opening with *God* makes the poem sound as if it is going to be more conventionally religious than *A Prayer for My Daughter* (p.27), but you may ask to whom it is addressed: is it *God*, or is the line aimed at one who overhears the poet musing with himself:

 3 **song** this could either mean a life that is fulfilled or a good work of art that will be read by future generations.

 4 **marrow-bone** in *Adam's Curse* this meant the knees; here it refers to bodily existence and to a life lived according to the passions of flesh and blood. You may catch a hint in this of those collectivist political theories that stressed impulse and physical energy rather than the life of the mind.

 6 **all** Yeats is still thinking about his relationship with his audience. See *The Fisherman* (p.19).

 8 **fool** the juxtaposition of the *fool* and the wise man is an ancient idea that has a religious significance.

 12 A characteristically Yeatsian phrase; see also *In Memory of Major Robert Gregory*, p.14 line 32. Think about the effect of yoking together two powerful adjectives: does this expand the meaning, sharply define the meaning, intensify the emotional

impact, heighten the reader's sense of the poet striving for effect or introduce a strained note! It can, of course, be a number of these.

from *New Poems*

Lapis Lazuli

Yeats was once given an intricately carved piece of lapis lazuli, a luminously blue and delicately veined stone which was highly valued (more so than gold) in the ancient world, and which may have been the basis for some of the images in this poem.

Yeats was interested in sculpture, often using it, as in *The Living Beauty* (p.18), as a metaphor for art. The poem he wrote about it has a fragmentary quality; reading it, we move from image to image without the help of connecting explanations. But given the subject – the creative life of the imagination – such a form is not surprising; we are implicitly invited to submit to the images as they unfold before us and allow those images to form pictures, thoughts, and feelings in our minds. Because of this several lines can be read in different ways. The words *Heaven blazing into the head* (19) can mean collapse and disintegration, or the illumination that comes from a vision. Perhaps such ambiguity is a sign that Yeats' imagination is at work, joyfully and playfully creating meaning upon meaning.

2 It is typical of Yeats that he talks of art through specific objects: *palette* for painting and *fiddle-bow* for music.

3 **gay** the word suggests a blithe, light-hearted, innocent and celebratory joy. There is no hint of the more recent association with homosexuality. See Approaches p.129.

4 **For everybody knows** the way *hysterical women* (1) speak?

6 **Zeppelin** a German airship used for bombing Britain in the First World War.

7 **King Billy** William of Orange who fought and defeated James II at the Battle of the Boyne. See *Pardon, Old Fathers* p.27 lines 10–12. See Approaches p.132.

9–11 *Ophelia* appears in Shakespeare's *Hamlet*, and *Cordelia* in his *King Lear*; both women come to tragic ends. See Approaches p.100.

17 Is the focus here on the players performing the parts or on the characters themselves understood as real people? If the former, then artists know that whatever is the subject of art, art itself is transfiguringly gay. If the latter, then the idea is that in tragedy the soul is enriched rather than crushed. The references to the theatre (9–24) might support the first view; the generalizing force of 18–22 the second.

29 **Callimachus** celebrated sculptor of ancient Greece, all of whose work has probably been destroyed.

33 **lamp-chimney** probably a reference to one of *Callimachus'* public buildings in Athens.

35–6 It is important to decide the tone of these lines because in their epigrammatic succinctness, they encapsulate the thought of the poem. Does the poet contemplate the rise and fall of things with sadness, indifference, detachment, acceptance or wonder?

40 **longevity** living a long life.

42 **musical instrument** perhaps Yeats does not say which *instrument* because he wants us to do what he does – work upon these images with our imagination (see 51–2).

45 **seems** the word might point to the way the poet's imagination helps to recreate the lapis lazuli figures so that they seem to be symbols of art.

An Acre of Grass

Does this poem about old age have the sad regretfulness or the bitter resentment of some of the other late poems, or is the tone one of repose and an acceptance of limitations? Thinking over this question, you should weigh the lines about *William Blake* (16–18) and the word *frenzy* (13, 21) with the peace of the opening image and the statement that the poet's *temptation is quiet* (7).

1–6 What is the effect of these note-like jottings? Do they show the weariness of age or a mind carefully selecting the important (and symbolic?) details of the scene?

7 **temptation** sexual or mental? *Loose* in 9 might point to the former, while line 10 may indicate the latter.

11 **rag and bone** see *The Circus Animals' Desertion* p.47 line 40.

15 Both *Timon* of Athens and King *Lear* (central characters in

Shakespearian plays) rage against old age and the folly and cruelty of the world.

16 **William Blake**   the English poet and artist (1757–1827) who had an intense belief in the power of the imagination to search out and even to create truth. See *Under Ben Bulben* p.49 line 65.

19 **Michael Angelo**   the Italian painter, sculptor, architect and poet (1475–1564) who painted the scene of the Last Judgement – *Shake the dead* (22) – on the walls of the Sistine Chapel in the Vatican. See *Under Ben Bulben* p.49 lines 45–52.

24 **eagle mind**   a pose, or the insight that with age there comes an eagle-like clarity of mind?

The Spur

This poem has spirit and zest but it is not easy to characterize its tone: is it that of a desperate man who is striving to be honest about his feelings, or is there guilt (or even surprise) that *lust and rage* are (1) still present? And what does he *lust* for and *rage* against? *Lust* is probably sexual desire, but *rage* is less easy to interpret; it could be against the folly of a politics that is leading to war, a nation unconcerned about its cultural heritage or a society unwilling to listen to the poet. A further possibility is that Yeats is chiefly interested in the experience of *lust and rage* (1) rather than their objects. Finally, you might ask yourself whether there is a deliberately playful flaunting of emotions that is out of keeping with old age. See Approaches pp.128–9.

The Municipal Gallery Revisited

In this retrospective work the poet dwells on concerns that have appeared in earlier poems. Like *In Memory of Major Robert Gregory* (p.14) it is a poem about friends, and how the poet comes to an understanding of himself through them. It is also a poem about Ireland; the pictures are of those people who, in the poet's view, gave Ireland its identity. Another familiar feature of the poem is the poet's presentation of himself as a poet, surrounded by those things which, in his own way, he creates: *images* (1). What is notable about the poem is its ease and conversational nonchalance; this is all the more remarkable because its subject matter is something that is not natural: art and images.

1–10 Does the terse, summary form of the writing about the pictures increase or decrease their importance? The singling out of details might point to their importance, but the clipped, glancing style could indicate that the poet regards them as less significant than ones later in the poem that are spoken of at greater length. See *Approaches* p.102.

3 **Casement** Sir Roger *Casement* (1864–1916) was tried, found guilty and executed for treason a few weeks after the executions of those involved in the Easter Rising.

4 **Griffith** Arthur *Griffith* (1871–1922) founded Sinn Fein, a political party dedicated to securing independence for Ireland. Because he felt that all art should serve the cause of Irish nationalism, he criticized playwrights such as J.M. Synge, whose picture of Ireland was not idealized.

5 **Kevin O'Higgins** Irish Minister of Justice. See *Death* (p.35).

10–12 See *Approaches* pp.111–2.

11 **dead Ireland** is the Ireland of the poet's youth dead in the sense that it is past and has been replaced by a newer Ireland, or is it dead because it is lifeless, sterile and unproductive?

12 **terrible and gay** for *terrible* see *Easter 1916* p.23 line 16 and for *gay Lapis Lazuli* p.41 line 3. See also *Approaches* p.132.

13 See *Approaches* p.105.

12–16 Perhaps the elegantly inventive rhyme *ago/studio* (15/16) hints at how the lady should be imagined.

17–19 See *Approaches* p.102.

20 The poet here identifies the *images* as his (note the use of *my*). This can be understood as those that appear in his poems and would include, for instance, those of Lady Gregory and Synge; but which then are the *impermanent* ones? Might Yeats be distinguishing between artistic and political figures?

21 **Hugh Lane** see *Coole Park, 1929* p.35 line 14.

22 **'onlie begetter'** a quotation from the dedication to Shakespeare's *Sonnets* where a 'Mr W. H.' is described as the *'onlie begetter'* of the *Sonnets*.

23 **Hazel Lavery** wife of the painter Sir John Lavery. She had died the year before the poem was written. There are two pictures of her in the Gallery.

25 **Mancini's portrait**   Antonio Mancini, an Italian artist who
painted Lady Gregory.

Augusta Gregory   friend, supporter and fellow worker with
Yeats in the establishment of an Irish Theatre. Coole Park, her
house, was sold and demolished after her death (37). See *Coole
Park, 1929*, (p.35) *Coole Park and Ballylee, 1931* (p.37), and
Approaches pp.117–8.

26 **Rembrandt**   the Dutch artist (1606–69) who is often spoken
of as the greatest of all portrait painters. Such lavish praise for
Mancini's portrait might be thought excessive.

John Synge   the playwright, poet and friend of Yeats. See *In
Memory of Major Robert Gregory* p.14 lines 25–32.

28–9 Yeats might be touching on the tension between the achieve-
ment of an impersonal art and the warm actuality of life. See
Sailing to Byzantium (p.30) and *Byzantium* (p.38).

33 **medieval knees**   Yeats loved traditional courtesy and felt it
was important to honour what he admired. See Approaches
pp.125–6.

39–40 The image of a place incapable of being desecrated because its
past occupants were inherently honourable is drawn, as the
poem says, from *The Ruins of Time* (216–7) by Edmund Spenser
(1555–99).

44 **Antaeus-like**   in classical mythology *Antaeus* was a giant who
was strong so long as he touched the earth. See Approaches
p.120.

47 A crucial line in Yeats. See *Under Ben Bulben* p.49 lines 75–8
and Approaches p.124.

from *Last Poems*

Long-Legged Fly

The strange thing about this enticing and mysterious poem is that
whilst it appears to be dealing with important matters, some of the
actions it mentions are insignificant. Its subject is the reveries of
three figures of legendary stature, and the tone might be said to be
awed and still; yet of those figures one has his eyes on *nothing* (7),
while another practises *a tinker shuffle* (17). One way into the poem

is to puzzle over its title and the intriguing refrain: might there be the suggestion that it needs the delicacy of a long-legged fly to probe the silence over which their minds move? There may be an important point about both art and life here: greatness does not come from weighty deliberation but from an essentially playful and even apparently insignificant (in literature flies are often symbols of what is passing and trivial) movement of the mind. See Approaches pp.121–2.

5 **Caesar** presumably Julius Caesar (102–44 BC), the Roman general who, after many conquests, became sole governor of the Roman provinces. You might ask what things he stands for: one is probably the safety of the realm. Are there others?

9–10 It is worth thinking about how this refrain (and other parts of the poem) presents moving on the surface not as superficial but as the sign of something important. See Approaches p.110.

10 **moves** perhaps an echo of the opening chapter of *Genesis* (the first book of *The Bible*), where, in the story of the creation, the Spirit of God moves *on the face of the waters* (*Genesis*. 1:2).

11 **topless towers** in Christopher Marlowe's play, *Dr Faustus*, Helen of Troy is said to have caused the burning of *the topless towers of Ilium* (Troy). Is it possible here to decide whether she stands for the heroism of legendary wars or for love and romance?

17 **tinker shuffle** a dance of the common people rather than one performed by lords and ladies.

22 **first Adam** here the name *Adam* probably stands for ordinary flesh and blood existence; that is to say, for people's sexual desires, passions and feelings.

23 **Pope's chapel** *Michael Angelo* (26) painted the Sistine chapel in the Vatican for the Pope. One of the paintings was of the creation of Adam, whom Michael Angelo boldly portrayed as naked.

26 **Michael Angelo** see *An Acre of Grass* p.43 line 19 and *Ben Bulben* p.49 lines 45–9.

The Circus Animals' Desertion

Because of this poem's similarity to *The Municipal Gallery Revisited* (p.44), think about what the poems have in common and whether there are differences in focus and subject matter. Related to these matters is the issue of tone: both poems have the attractive nonchalance and relaxed conversational air of later Yeats, but in this poem there are passages which you might find brooding and troubled. This may be because Yeats is pondering the nature of his art – what he finds attractive and what he feels is the source of his inspiration. The problem he confronts is that although he found images absorbing in themselves, irrespective of the relations they established with actual life, he recognizes that their source is his murky self, *the foul rag-and-bone shop of the heart* (40). This may be the most powerful tension in the whole of Yeats' poetry. His original titles were 'Despair' and 'On the Lack of a Theme'. See Approaches p.120.

1 **sought** does the repeated *sought* enhance the searching and probing sense of the poem, or does the use of the past tense enable the reader to see that the poet has found a theme? See Approaches p.128.

4 **heart** what are the associations of *heart*, particularly when used in poetry, and are they significantly different in this poem?

10 **Oisin** Yeats's first major poem, published in 1889, was *The Wandering of Oisin*. The mythical hero, *Oisin*, travels to three islands. Niamh, with whom he falls in love, carried him on her horse across the sea to fairyland.

11 **allegorical dreams** an allegory is a literary work in which every character or event corresponds directly to an element in a philosophical or religious system. It is worth noting that Yeats does not say of what Oisin's wanderings are allegorical.

16 **faery bride** although no name is given, the figure of Maud Gonne is unavoidable.

18 **The Countess Cathleen** a play written by Yeats in 1899. Maud Gonne played the Countess. The plot, as indicated in lines 19–21, concerns a woman who, for the sake of the starving people, offers to sell her soul to the Devil in exchange for bread.

22 Compare *A Prayer for My Daughter* p.27 lines 57–64.

25–6 Characters from Yeats' play *On Baile's Strand* (1904). The hero, *Cuchulain*, dies fighting the sea.

31–2 See Approaches pp.131–2.

35–8 See Approaches p.107.

38–40 The ladder is a much used image for progress in art or thought. These lines provoke a number of questions: does *must* (39) indicate determination, a forced but reluctant action, or an action carried out willingly? There is also the question of whether the poet recoils from the realization that the sources of his imagination are *foul* (40) or whether he welcomes (and even relishes?) the (liberating?) idea that his *masterful images* (33) are related to the dark (but vigorous?) life of the self.

Politics

The quotation from the novelist and intellectual Thomas Mann (1875–1955) implies that the responsible artist should be concerned with political issues. It was another intellectual, the American poet and critic Archibald MacLeish, who prompted Yeats to write the poem when he praised Yeats for being a politically aware poet. Yeats' dramatic response covers many of his concerns: the public role of the poet (it is addressed to a bystander who appears to think that poets should engage with contemporary issues); the competing demands of reason and passion; a high romantic love that adores and longs for a beloved from a distance, and the bitter resentment of old age. Is it a political poem? See Approaches pp.103–4.

3 **Roman**   probably a reference to Mussolini's fascist Italy.
  Russian   probably Stalin's communist Russia.
4 **Spanish**   several English poets volunteered to fight in the Spanish Civil War (1936–9).
10 **war's alarms**   the poem was written in 1938, when the likelihood of war was increasing.
11 **O**   should this be read as a passionate outburst or as a subdued whisper? The bold, romantic stance of the poem would seem to suggest the former, but given the implication that the poet really ought to be interested in politics, a quiet, slightly shamed reading might be truer to the tone of the poem.

Under Ben Bulben

Ben Bulben, a mountain north of Sligo rising to fifteen hundred feet, was known to Yeats from his boyhood. Although Yeats wrote poems after this one, it deliberately presents itself as a weaving together of his poetic concerns (he thought of calling it 'Creed' or

'Convictions') and it is often placed last in collections of his verse. It is, so to speak, Yeats' poetic last will and testament. The final lines were used as the epitaph on his grave in Drumcliff churchyard. As a poem about the achievements of a life it recalls *In Memory of Major Robert Gregory* (p.14) and *The Municipal Gallery Revisited* (p.44), but whereas in those poems Yeats used a dignified ten-syllable line that creates and is expressive of the gravity and magnificence of the lives he is celebrating, in *Under Ben Bulben* the line is short (usually seven syllables), and rather than being grand and elevating is punchy, robust, and at times, blunt. Some critics compare it to a magic chant or charm. It is worth remembering that in social terms, a long line is associated with cultured and aristocratic subjects, whereas poetry written by and about the common people often uses short lines. See Approaches p.109.

When faced with a poem that strives to be, in the words of the American critic, Ivor Winters, *a final statement*, readers might feel they have to judge what it says, if only because to do otherwise would be patronizing and untrue to the poem's status as an assertion of belief. Can a reader believe what this poem says; that is to say, can a reader accept reincarnation (13–24) and the virtue of being *fighting mad* (28)? A way round this, as with many Yeats poems, is to see these things as symbols of the working of the imagination, so reincarnation becomes the recurrence of images, and violence the frenzy of the imagination. Another way of coming to terms with this question is to read the poem as a set of metaphors about achieving a full life, be that a life of action or art.

Is the tone powerful, thrusting, honest, sincere and brave, or a blend of rant, bluster and self-absorbed posturing?

1–4   *The sages* (wise men) and *the Witch of Atlas* (a figure in a poem by Shelley who symbolizes wisdom) are spiritual authorities. *The Mareotic Lake* in upper Egypt was associated with early Christian monastic life; here it seems to stand for a remote place, where sages contemplate the true nature of God and humanity. Who is to *swear*: all people, the Irish poets, the readers? It could also be the poet's way of saying: I *swear*.

5–11 The *horsemen* are probably the ghostly riders which were said to gallop over Ben Bulben. What might their inclusion as authorities indicate? Perhaps line 16 helps.

12 **gist** is the *gist* (an appropriately pithy word?) found in lines 23–4 or in the rest of the poem?

14–15 The poem appears to assume the eternity of the soul but sees it in terms of *two eternities* (14): race or culture, and the life of the individual soul.

24 **human mind** see the discussion in the headpiece about reincarnation. Another possibility is that it means that what interested one mind now interests another.

25 **Mitchel's prayer** John *Mitchel* (1815–75), an Irish nationalist who, in his Jail Journal, altered the words of the prayer *Give peace in our time, O Lord* to *Give us war in our time, O Lord*.

30 **completes** a central word in the poem.

36 **mate** the violence the poet revels in is also sexual.

37–83 See Approaches pp.127–8.

37 **work** the implication is that it is the same kind of *work* that is done by *the sages* (1) and those who practise violence.

38–9 Lines that should be recalled when thinking about the place of tradition in Yeats' thought.

42 **Measurement** the kind of art that is praised in *The Living Beauty* (p.18).

43 **stark Egyptian** probably the philosopher Plotinus (205–70 AD) who speculated about the relationship between God and the visible world. He thought that artists looked through nature to the eternal forms that alone are real.

44 **Phidias** the Greek sculptor who worked on the Parthenon in Athens.

45 **Michael Angelo** painted the creation of Adam on the *roof* of the *Sistine Chapel* in the Vatican. See *Long-Legged Fly* p.46 lines 21–8.

51 A paradox: how can *perfection* be *profane* (worldly and irreligious)?

52 **Quattrocento** fifteenth-century Italian art. See *Among School Children* p.32 line 26.

62 **Gyres** cycles or phases of history. See *The Second Coming* p.26 line 1.

65 **Calvert** Edward *Calvert* (1799–1883), an English landscape painter whose work has a visionary glow.

Wilson Richard *Wilson* (1714–82), a landscape painter who idealized his subjects by filling them with light.

Blake William *Blake* (1757–1827) was a visionary poet and artist. See *An Acre of Grass* p.43 line 16.

Claude   *Claude* Lorrain (1600–82), a French painter noted for radiant sunsets.

67   **Palmer's phrase**   Samuel *Palmer* (1805–81) was a visionary English painter who presented the landscape of southern England as an earthly paradise.

74–7   The issue of the ideal audience emerges here; see notes to *The Fisherman* on pp.66–7.

85   **Drumcliff**   a village at the foot of Ben Bulben. (See 'Pardon, Old Fathers' p.9 lines 5–8 and *September 1913* p.10 line 21.)

86   **an ancestor**   the Rev'd John Yeats (1774–1846) was Rector of Drumcliff for over thirty years. (See September 1913 p.10 lines 5–8.)

90–4   See Approaches p.127.

92   **cold**   the most crucial word in the poem? In order to understand it, readers should ignore the usual associations of frigidity and lifelessness and think how the poems often admire art that is impersonal. See Approaches pp.126–7.

94   **Horseman**   what importance can be attached to the fact that the poem opens and closes with horsemen? Should you, for instance, see those at the end as similar to or different from those at the start of the poem, and what are the consequences of your conclusion?

Approaches

Approaches Through Poetic Language

The Voice of Yeats

People who enjoy reading Yeats often say things like this: 'I don't always understand what he's saying but I like the sound of his voice'. It is his voice that has led readers to him. Quite often critics praise him for the strangely beautiful music or his incantations; W. W. Robson has called him a *lord of language, of Shakespearian splendour* who *sang*. What Robson might have had in mind are openings such as this one from *A Prayer for My Daughter*:

> Once more the storm is howling, and half hid
> Under this cradle-hood and coverlid
> My child sleeps on. (1–3)

What do you hear in those lines? Two of the things that you may be conscious of are the strong presence of a speaking voice and emphatic (but not heavy or clumsy) rhythms. Let us think about these two things in more detail.

When reading Yeats, we are aware of him as a speaker. Sometimes he calls attention to the act of speaking; in *The Cold Heaven* (p.11), for instance, he says (and you can feel it in the movement of the verse) *I cried and trembled* (8). His speech is often accompanied by implicit gestures; in *Lapis Lazuli* (p.41), for instance, he directs the reader (note the use of *there* and *that*) to Shakespeare's tragic heroes and heroines as if he too were sharing the stage with them: *There struts Hamlet, there is Lear, | That's Ophelia, that Cordelia* (10–11). Yeats himself said that a poet is someone who *has stepped out of a play*.

Yeats' rhythms have been described above as emphatic: what makes them so? One of the factors is where the stress falls. It is common in English for the rhythm to move towards a stress, so of two syllables it is often the second rather than the first that is emphasized. Yeats does write like this, but there are many occasions when the poem, or one of its lines, opens powerfully with a stressed syllable. A *Prayer for My Daughter* (p.27) opens with the (equally!) strong *Once more*, and in *Lapis Lazuli* (p.41) *There* and *That's* are both firmly stressed.

A second feature that gives Yeats this attractively forceful and assertive quality is what I am going to call the presence of the poet in the rhythms of the poem. Here I think it is helpful to consider the argument of a contemporary Irish poet, Seamus Heaney. In a thought-provoking lecture called *The Making of a Music* (in *Preoccupations* see Further Reading p.140), Heaney argues that while Wordsworth surrendered to the rhythmic possiblities of his ideas, Yeats tried to control and discipline them. Heaney says we have to think of Yeats testing and trying out different voices and deciding on which will come most resonantly, and he writes of composition for Yeats as being *a mastery, a handling, a struggle towards maximum articulation*. You might ask yourself whether this suggestion does justice to your sense of the verse. Do you find Yeats ordering, shaping, fixing and giving a final form to his thought and feelings? If so, you can speak of Yeats as present in his poems as a poet who directs and places words in his effort to achieve a full articulation. This, to underline the main point of this section, is something that can be heard in *A Deep-Sworn Vow*:

Others because you did not keep
That deep-sworn vow have been friends of mine;
Yet always when I look death in the face,
When I clamber to the heights of sleep,
Or when I grow excited with wine,
Suddenly I meet your face.   (1–6)

This is a very emotional poem, yet the first statement unfolds with the deliberateness of someone wanting speech to be unambiguous and exact. The poet might be imagined as establishing control by pushing forward the temperate word *friends* as a counterweight to the more emotionally resonant phrase *deep-sworn vow*. In the third line he arrests the movement momentarily on the evenly balanced *always*, before releasing in the fifth line a word which, at last, is in keeping with the mounting tension – *excited*. Perhaps this example has shown that Yeats sometimes seeks to control and sometimes submits to the emotional and intellectual impulses that flow through his verse. One of the exciting things about reading him is that this can be heard in the voices of the poems.

What Kind of Voice?

We have already gone some way towards answering this question. Yeats' voice is an assertive and emphatic one that seeks to control and shape what is being said. There is, however, more to say: Yeats is a dramatic poet. Although the words of a poet about his or her own work should always be treated with care (they might be of very great interest but can never be of overriding authority), it is significant that Yeats drew attention to his own practice of dramatizing himself:

> Even now and then, when something has stirred my imagination,
> I begin talking to myself. I speak in my own person and dramatize
> myself...
>
> Quoted in *Preoccupations*

These words make sense of the poems: the manner in which the poet places himself in a scene, makes gestures and audibly strives to control what he is saying are all ways in which the essentially dramatic nature of Yeats' poetry is realized. *The Municipal Gallery Revisited* (p.44) opens with a sweeping, all-embracing gesture as the poet indicates where he is: *Around me the images of thirty years* (1) and his emotional reaction to the pictures is given particular emphasis: *Heart-smitten with emotion I sink down,/My heart recovering with covered eyes* (17–18). *Heart-smitten* (17) is powerful, not least because of the old-fashioned quality of the word *smitten*; the second line draws attention to itself by the deliberate play upon *recovering* and *covered* (18) and the (slightly stagey?) gesture of shielding the eyes as an indication of strong emotional feeling.

The poems are also dramatic in the way in which they exhibit changes in their emotional and intellectual life. One of the invigorating things about Yeats is the constantly changing pulse of his poems; moreover, it is this pulse that creates the sense of a man thinking and feeling his way through a poem. As a result, the rhythmical life of each poem avoids stilted regularity; the poems demand to be read as authentic expressions of actual thinking and feeling.

It is a useful exercise to try to be precise about the exact character of Yeats' voice. Words such as 'noble' 'lofty', 'proud', 'oratorical' and 'magniloquent' (high sounding and ambitious) might well be used; the critic, Middleton Murray, spoke of his *high and passionate argument*, and the contemporary critic, Denis Donoghue, called the blend of elevated language and disciplined control an *equestrian authority* (an appropriate image given the importance of the horse in a poem such as *Under Ben Bulben* (p.49). Perhaps none of these formulations is as impressive as Yeats' own *excited reverie* in *A Prayer for My Daughter* (p.27) line 13.

But the Yeats voice has also attracted criticism. Heaney says of Yeats' language that, at its worst, it is *bragging*. F. R. Leavis praised Yeats for being in touch with *the living language* and *the speaking voice* but he diagnosed what he felt was a characteristically Irish failing, *that habit of cultivating attitudes and postures...* (*Lectures in America*, see Further Reading p.140). Both Heaney and Leavis are on to something here; there is a theatrical element in Yeats which involves the danger of posing and posturing, of self-consciously striking an attitude and swaggering before his audience. A reader might judge this theatricality as bluster, pomposity and portentousness. How, for instance, do you respond to *'Pardon, Old Fathers'* (p.9)? Questions such as this often occur when reading Yeats: are you impressed by the passion and energy of his voice or irritated by his posturing?

Activity

In the light of the above discussion of Yeats' voice, read *Politics* (p.48) and consider what questions and issues it raises.

Discussion

The poem opens with the poet making a dramatic gesture in the direction of the girl, who is *standing there* (1). The fact that the poet asks a rhetorical question inevitably draws our attention to *his* plight. You may be impressed by the anguish of the old man who longs for physical love, or find the parading of emotions embarrassing. In the unexpected rhyme of *fix/politics* (2/4) you might sense the poet strenuously shaping (fixing?) his language in order to make clear to himself the issues of love, war and age. The close of the poem raises the issue of posturing: is this a case of the poet posing as a would-be lover, or can you read it as an outburst of real passion, which is made particularly poignant by the age of the poet and the intellectual pressure upon him to think about the world in political terms?

Word Order

Yeats' voice is one of the functions of his language. More specifically, it is partly the creation of his word order. One of the remarkable things about the poetry of Yeats is that it underwent a considerable change in his middle years. *Adam's Curse* (p.5) marks a turning point with its closeness to ordinary speech. The first time the poet speaks there is a musing, off-hand quality created by a casual *maybe* at the end of the line: *I said, 'A line will take us hours maybe'* (4). It sounds (and is meant to) like easy after-dinner conversation. Contractions of words such as *There's* (16) and *It's* (21) contribute to the conversational air.

But what chiefly distinguishes Yeats' style is neither the deployment of the casual word at the close of a phrase nor the use of contractions, but his adoption of standard, as opposed to a deliberately 'poetic', word order. One of the things that has distinguished English poetry is the way poets have rearranged natural word order. This can be very effective, not least because the rearrangement draws readers' attention to the crafted and composed nature of art. Readers of poetry become accustomed to these deliberate departures from ordinary word order and so when they read a poet who follows speech rather than rearranging it, there is the pleasure of surprise and, perhaps, the greater pleasure of finding that art – something that is usually out of the ordinary – can be made out of quite ordinary forms of speech.

This quality is best seen through contrast. In the early poem, *The Lake Isle of Innisfree* (p.2), Yeats inverts natural word order when he speaks of *the pavements grey* (11) instead of *the grey pavements*. Later, however, poems are, to quote Leavis once more, *in touch with the spoken living language*. Notice how the opening of *An Irish Airman Foresees His Death* is direct and even conversational: *I know that I shall meet my fate/Somewhere among the clouds above* (1–2).

But Yeats does employ rhetorical strategies – deliberately shaped ways of speaking – consciously, to create effects. If it suits his purposes, he departs from the word orders of speech. When in *The Municipal Gallery Revisited* he says, *Before a woman's portrait suddenly I stand* (13), the unexpected placing of *suddenly* throws more stress on the effect the portrait has upon him.

Another Yeatsian practice is the compression of lines by omitting words. Take, for example, this line from *Lapis Lazuli: All men have aimed at, found and lost* (18). If we spelt out the meaning by including the omitted words we would have something like this: All that men have aimed at, all the things, that is, that they have aimed at and then found and afterwards lost. Sometimes Yeats is difficult, and one of the reasons for this is his compressions. But there are compensations: Yeats' lines, as in the case of the one just quoted, can sound economical and assertive because of their terse quality.

Yeats also shaped his lines by balancing words. *In Memory of Major Robert Gregory* (p.14) contains these lines about the poet and playwright Synge:

And that enquiring man John Synge comes next,
That dying chose the living world for text
And never could have rested in the tomb
But that, long travelling, he had come
Towards nightfall upon certain set apart   (25–9)

The passage is built up on a set of balancing words and phrases: *dying/living* (26), *rested/travelling* (27, 28), that draw attention to the moulded character of the writing.

Those lines also exemplify Yeats' practice of building qualifications, usually in the form of subordinate clauses, into his poems. The effect created is that of being directly in touch with the author's thinking as it happens. The inclusion above of the qualificatory *long travelling* (28) shows that the poet is alert to the (costly?) commitment of seeking *certain* (another compression, meaning certain people) *set apart* (29). Often Yeats' most important lines appear as afterthoughts; see, for instance, the last three lines of *The Magi* (p.11).

Yeats repeats words. Repetition focuses the reader's attention upon the art of the poet, the fact that it is something made rather than just occurring naturally. Repetition also enriches the meaning of the repeated word. The words *balanced* and *balance* (13, 16) in *An Irish Airman Foresees His Death* (p.18) are an example of this.

A similar feature is Yeats' use of the rhetorical question. Because the function of a rhetorical question is not to find an answer, but to alert the listener to the issue that concerns the speaker, it usually has the effect of drawing attention to both the one who speaks and the act of speaking. *No Second Troy* (p.7) is comprised of four sentences, all of them rhetorical questions. The effect is that, as so often happens in Yeats, the poem is as much about the poet as the person who is the 'true' subject.

A final way in which word order creates distinctive effects is the occasional use of the interjection. Yeats is not afraid of using the traditional poetic exclamation O, as in *O when may it suffice?* (59) from *Easter 1916*. The remarkable thing for a poet who, for all the careful rhetorical shaping of his language, strove for a modern sounding speech in touch with the spoken word, is that he uses the O quite traditionally to indicate the swelling of an emotion.

Activity

In the light of the above discussion read the third stanza of *Coole Park and Ballylee, 1931* (p.37) and consider its rhetorical strategies. There are examples of every sort with the exception of the interjection.

Discussion

By altering the expected word order from *That stormy white/Seems but* to *That stormy white/But seems* (17–18), Yeats throws the emphasis upon the word *But* and thereby underscores the illusory quality of the sight. In the third line he puts in the qualification *like the soul* (19), which shows that here, as elsewhere in the poem, he is aware that his mind is seeking to make connections. The qualification, as so often in ordinary speech, appears before the main subject. The main subject itself is a neatly balanced picture of a transitory scene which sails into sight and is gone in the morning. Another carefully weighted balance is the one in the fifth and sixth lines where the near repetition of *sets to right* (21) and *set awry* (22) shows how the *emblem* (17) restores a balance that had been lost.

Individual Words

Yeats' later poetry departs from self-consciously 'poetic' diction. The poet himself said that he tried to make the language of poetry akin to that of *passionate, normal speech*. Again, the contrast can be drawn by looking at *The Lake Isle of Innisfree* (p.2). In that poem there are moments when the words are deployed with the atmospheric sweep of an impressionist painter's brush-strokes:

> for peace comes dropping slow,
> Dropping from the veils of the morning to where the cricket sings;
> There midnight's all a glimmer, and noon a purple glow,   (5–7)

The soft consonants and vowels, the mesmeric repetitions, the words that evoke muted light, those that deal with the sounds of nature and those that denote exotic colour are all unmistakably 'poetic'. The later Yeats is very different:

> A mound of refuse or the sweepings of a street,
> Old kettles, old bottles, and a broken can,
> Old iron, old bones, old rags, that raving slut
> Who keeps the till.   (35–8)

These words from *The Circus Animals' Desertion* (p.47) refer to what is squalid and negligible; furthermore, they have a colloquial tang – *that raving slut* (37). Above all, they are not the kind of words that are popularly associated with poetry.

Yeats' diction, particularly in the later poems, is often mixed. For example, in the sixth stanza of *Among School Children* (p.32) there are the following varied words: *spume* (41) – an almost technical word for the froth that gathers on disturbed water; *paradigm* (42) – an intellectual model; *taws* (43) – an old word for a leather strap; *bottom* (44) in its anatomical sense; *fiddle-stick* (46) – a colloquial word for violin, and *Muses* (47) – the inspirers of poetry in Greek mythology. One of the things you must be alert to when reading Yeats is this rapid shifting from one language level to another. It creates added excitement; we feel we are in the presence of the poet as he moves from one level to another in his quest to be true to the constantly changing nature of his thinking and feeling.

One of Yeats' reasons for moving from one level to another may well have been his ambition to write with precision. Certainly

Yeats, like most poets, works by exploiting the potential ranges of meaning in words, but the overall impression the reader usually has of his poetic diction is one of pin-point accuracy. We feel that he is being both insightful and truthful when he writes in *The People* (p.20) of his virtues being *the definitions/Of the analytic mind* (32–3). A poet who values precision will be likely to use the formal *definitions* (32) and will not be afraid of sounding cold when he chooses the adjective *analytic* (33) – exact and incisive – to bring out the chief function of the mind. W. W. Robson characterized Yeats' diction as being at once *both surprising and inevitable*. These qualities are, I believe, a function of his striving for accuracy. The words *definitions* and *analytic* are not what we might expect in a poem about the public role of a poet, but, once used, we can see how they focus his discriminating and critical search for scrupulous poetic precision. They surprise us, convince us of their rightness, and, we may add, delight us by revealing the poet's disciplined art. This is specially true of the short poems, which often derive their impact from the strategic use of a single word; think, for instance, of *glittered* in the last line of *To A Young Girl* (p.19).

Activity

In the light of the foregoing discussion, read stanzas three and four of *A Prayer for My Daughter* (p.27) and think about the different kinds of words Yeats uses.

Discussion

The word *sufficient* (21) in the third stanza has a logical function. It means not merely that which is necessary but that which will fully perform a task. In using it, Yeats is unambiguously asserting that beauty can never be the full purpose or goal of any person. In the fourth stanza there are some significant changes in language level. *Flat and dull* (25) and *could have her way* (28) are conversational, even slangy, expressions; both are different from the mythical *Horn of Plenty* (32). In such shifts we can see the carefully balanced estimation Yeats makes of beautiful women; he attempts to reduce their power by using colloquial phrases of them but cannot exclude the elevating language of myth when speaking of their capricious (wilfully changeable) taste.

Poetic Form

The emphasis so far has been on Yeats the disciplined craftsman, who controls his rhythm and diction. Another way of exerting control is through form. In many respects Yeats is a traditional poet. In the Twentieth century many poets have chosen to write 'free verse', verse that avoids regular rhythms and rhyme and has lines of varying length. Yeats did not take up that option; he was concerned with the regulation and patterning of his poetry. Four areas are of interest in this respect: type or genre, stanza shape, rhyme, and his use of the refrain.

Although Yeats rarely titled his poems to indicate it, he did write in many of the traditional genres. For instance, *In Memory of Major Robert Gregory* is called neither an elegy (a poem of mourning) nor an ode (a highly wrought poem on a lofty subject), and yet it pays tribute to a dead hero and deals with the very elevated subject of the relationship between action and art. *The Mask* can be said to be a lyric, *Adam's Curse* a conversation poem, *Sixteen Dead Men* a kind of popular song, and *Leda and the Swan* a sonnet. Yeats is a poet who consciously writes within literary traditions.

Tradition is even more evident in the matter of Yeats' stanza. Yeats himself said: *I must choose a traditional stanza.* When writing the lofty, serious poems, he adopted the eight-line stanza with lines of ten syllables. In this stanza Yeats could be eloquent and emotionally flexible; he could pursue a logical argument and arouse and then allay strong feelings. These features and effects can be seen in poems such as *In Memory of Major Robert Gregory* and *A Prayer for My Daughter*. But Yeats should not be imagined as only working with traditional forms; in the same way in which each poem has its own rhythm or music, so many of his poems seem to evolve a form solely for their own purposes. *Under Ben Bulben*'s short, urgent and aggressive line is a case in point.

One of the expectations we have of poetry is rhyme; and Yeats does not disappoint us. Quite often his rhymes are so natural and unforced that they avoid the embarrassment that comes when a poet is straining to make words fit. He can also be inventive; in *Easter 1916* (p.23) he rhymes *argument* with *spent* (17/19). Increasingly, he used near-rhyme (sometimes called half-rhyme). This can create multiple effects. In the opening stanza of *Among School Children* (p.32) *replies/histories* (2/4) and *upon/man* (7/8) might suggest, the kind of casual ease that befits *A sixty-year-old smiling public man* (8) on a school visit. Because near-rhyme can sound less emphatic, its alternation with full rhyme can adjust the tension of a poem by relaxing it with a near-rhyme and increasing it with a full one; listen, for instance, to this effect in *Death* (p.35). A final thing to look out for in Yeats' handling of rhyme is the place it has in establishing the aphoristic force of some of his writing. An aphorism is a brief, compact and pithy saying. *The Spur* (p.43) is aphoristic, and perhaps something of its uncomfortable power derives from the near-rhyme of *young/song* (3/4) coming after a full rhyme that enacts the poem's subject matter, the *rage* of *age* (1/2).

Yeats' fondness for the refrain is a reminder that one of his roots, artistically speaking, is folk and ballad poetry. It is worth considering what he does with it. What, for instance, is to be made of the refrain to *Long-Legged Fly* (p.46): does it amplify what has gone before, undercut it with the thought that no human thinking can have the delicacy of the lightly skimming fly, or does it add an air of mystery because it is not obviously related to the subject matter?

Approaches Through the Life

Yeats and Ireland

I chose to start these Approaches with poetic language because, as we shall see later, being a poet was one of the chief subjects of Yeats' poetry. The risk of taking this line is that it can detach him from his setting. In order to avoid that, we shall turn to questions of history and biography.

Yeats was Irish. He was born in Dublin, and in 1947, eight years after his death (in France), his body was buried in Drumcliff churchyard beneath Ben Bulben. Moreover, he was a Senator of the Irish Free State and in his younger days he had worked with his friend Lady Gregory to establish an Irish theatrical tradition. His poems abound in references to the Irish countryside, Irish mythology, Irish history and contemporary Irish politics. But it is not quite as simple as that. Yeats was (and often felt himself to be), in some measure, out of the mainstream of Irish life. He was born into a Protestant and not, as the majority were, a Catholic family; English was his language rather than the traditional Gaelic, and for much of his early life he lived in London, only returning to Ireland for his holidays. For 57 of his 73 years Ireland, although enjoying a degree of administrative independence, was part of the United Kingdom. Two important features of his poetry can be looked at in the light of this: his quarrel with the Ireland that he knew, and his desire to create in his poetry an Ireland to which he would be proud to belong.

The Yeats that emerges in the poems is someone who was ambivalent about his country; that is to say, he had contrary feelings about it. Innisfree is a kind of earthly paradise which haunts the poet while he stands on desolate, grey city pavements, and Coole Park is an oasis of civilized life. But in *The People*, Dublin is *this unmannerly town*, and *September 1913* presents contemporary Ireland as the land where mean-spirited people *fumble in a greasy till*(2). The importance of these ambivalent feelings is that they help to define one of Yeats' chief interests – the relationship between poet and audience. Yeats is aware of himself as a poet, particularly as a poet who speaks, so it is of great concern to him that he has an audience who know how to listen. He said he admired certain eighteenth-century poets because they spoke or tried to speak *out of a people to a people*. Yeats wanted to speak out of and to the experience of the Irish people, yet was aware that they often did not listen.

Yeats' difficulty with his audience may be one of the motivating forces behind his desire to create an image of Ireland. Here, one of the emphases of contemporary criticism is of help. One of the interests of criticism today is the way authors create rather than reflect. There is much talk about how the act of writing brings ideas and values into being, rather than transcribes onto paper existing notions. In this respect Yeats can be said to be writing Ireland, bringing into being a world that he has imagined and made. Denis Donoghue put the point pithily: *Yeats*, he said, *invented a country, calling it Ireland*. This is one of his themes in *The Municipal Gallery Revisited* (p.44):

'This is not,' I say,
'The dead Ireland of my youth, but an Ireland
The poets have imagined...'   (10–12)

The lines play off the meanings of *dead* (11) and *imagined* (12); either *Ireland* was *dead* till it was *imagined*, or the *Ireland* that once existed has been replaced by the one the poets have brought into being through their imaginations. In a real sense, Ireland had to be imagined into existence – because of its links with the United Kingdom, it was not a separate nation. What image of Ireland, then, did Yeats create?

His Ireland has a geographical identity; look, for instance, at the landscape in *In Memory of Major Robert Gregory* (p.14). In this landscape people maintain a traditional way of life, in touch with the earth and nourished by folk memories. But for Yeats the cultural traditions that most matter are not the folk ones but those sustained by the great country houses, where a largely Protestant aristocracy maintained standards of literary and artistic sophistication. This is the theme of the Coole Park poems.

Ireland also has its heritage of poets – *Raftery* in *Coole Park and Ballylee, 1931* (4), *Synge* in *In Memory of Major Robert Gregory* (25–32), *Coole Park, 1929* (13), and *The Municipal Gallery Revisited* (40–55) – and politicians – *Wolfe Tone* in *September 1913* (21), and *Sixteen Dead Men* (16), *Edward Fitzgerald* in *September 1913* (20), and *Sixteen Dead Men* (16). Yeats' poetry is rich in the names of those he designates as the founders of Irish culture and history. '*Pardon, Old Fathers*' (p.9) presents the poet's own forebears as men who were adventurous, independent and admired – the kind of men upon whom a national tradition can be firmly built.

One way of thinking about what Yeats was doing is to see him creating a country in terms of the things that were then thought to define a nation – a beautiful countryside, a folk tradition, magnificent architecture, a memory of dramatic events that brought the nation into being, and a tradition of heroes and writers. Nationalism (of whatever nation) creates as well as discovers its past and present.

Yeats and the Easter Rising

One of the ways in which Yeats gives an identity to Ireland is by writing about the events that brought the Irish Free State into existence. *Easter 1916* (p.23) and *Sixteen Dead Men* (p.25) are his response to the Easter Rising, the series of events which can be seen as crucial for the foundation of modern Ireland. What happened as a result of Patrick Pearse taking over the Dublin Post Office is outlined in the notes to *Easter 1916* (see pp.69–71). As an event in itself it was not without absurdity; there was no way in which they could ever be successful, and more importantly, the majority of the Irish themselves were against a fight, not least because the Government had already promised to enact the bill granting independence once the war was over. What made the event a turning point was the quite aggressive reaction of the British and, as Yeats implies in *Easter 1916*, the way in which the sheer thrill of the action, for all its folly, captured and thereby also created, something essentially Irish – a wild gesture that excited in people the frenzied hope of liberation.

The achievement of *Easter 1916* is that Yeats manages to convey the dramatic change in thought and feeling – A *terrible beauty is born* (16, 40, 80) – and still remain aware of the human cost of what went on. He engages with the complexities of politics; the deaths might be *needless* (67) because *England may keep faith* (68). Above all, he dwells on what political involvement can do to people. In a long central section (41–56) he meditates on the *stone* (43) that troubles *the living stream* (44). The *stone*, like those who joined in the Rising, is hard, purposeful, resilient and stable, because it has *one purpose alone* (41) and does not, like *horse* (45), *rider* (46), *birds* (46) and the moving clouds, change *minute by minute* (48). But nor does it *live* (55). Witholding that word from the heroes of the Rising was brave of Yeats: in so acting, did they turn into fanatics who could not value that for which they were fighting?

Activity

Read lines 17–40 of *Easter 1916* (p.23) and make notes to show how Yeats' in his use of language seeks to preserve a balance between the achievement and the cost of the Easter Rising.

Discussion

Line 18 telescopes both possibilities into a single phrase – the woman is well intentioned but misled: *ignorant good-will*. The cost to her is dear and is heard in the way her voice, once *sweet* (21), has grown *shrill* (20); yet we may feel that the picture of her riding to *harriers* (23) is of no consequence in the world that has just been born. The observation that one of the men *was coming into his force* (27) prepares us for the recognition that his was a life of promise cut short: *He might have won fame in the end* (28). But is there just a hint that such a sentiment is out of keeping with the times, that it is part of a culture that has passed away? If this is so, the idea is very remarkable in a poem written during the First World War, when such thinking was both natural and consolatory.

Yeats, Women, and Love

Biographical criticism – reading an author's works in terms of his or her life – has not been popular in recent years. There is a good reason for this: the meaning of a literary work is made by its words, and so it follows that any words outside that work, such as a letter from the author explaining the work, cannot be finally authoritative. What the author has said outside the work is certainly of great interest, but it can never be a substitute for thinking about what the words actually say. A similar argument can be advanced about a literary work that arises out of an event in the author's life: knowledge of the event will no doubt be of great interest; nevertheless, the work will mean what it does because of the way its words work.

Having said that, one of the curious things about Yeats is the fact that he has invited a good deal of biographical criticism. The reason for this is that it is known that a good many of his poems originated in actual events. The challenge of Yeats, therefore, is to know what to do with this knowledge. If we are careful, we can use biographical material not as a guide to meaning, but as a context for discussing the poems. Whenever we discuss a poem we assume a context for it; it is possible to think of that context as an event that mattered to Yeats, because it was part of his life. More importantly, we can look at what Yeats made of the events in the poems. The chief interest that biography can have for the reader is as material that the poet has turned into art.

The most important relationship in Yeats' life was his hopeless pursuit of the Irish actress, Maud Gonne. He first met her in London in 1889, and it is known that he proposed to her at least six times. She always rejected him. In 1903 she married John MacBride, one of those who was shot in 1916 after the Easter Rising.

Of the poems in this selection at least twelve are in some way concerned with Maud Gonne. In keeping with the critical principle outlined above, we shall ask how Yeats presents the figure of the desired but unattainable woman. The first thing that should be said is that Yeats does not name her. She is, among other things, *the loveliest woman born* (59) in *A Prayer for My Daughter*, his *faery bride* (16) in *The Circus Animals' Desertion* and the woman with *A Ledaean body* (9), in *Among School Children*. Already we can see the objection to biographical criticism at work: do we need to know who stands behind these words, when the poet himself does not name her? If Maud Gonne matters at all, she matters as an image, formed, not unlike Yeats' image of Ireland, by the poems we meet on the page.

That this figure is a literary creation may be seen in the way great beauty is ascribed to her. It is virtually a convention of love poetry to write of the beloved as the most beautiful woman in the world. It is to Yeats' credit that he does not dodge this option; the one he loves (listen to the swell of wonder) is *the loveliest woman born*. Likewise, there is a tradition of presenting elusive beloveds as fairies – beautiful, alluring and potentially destructive creatures who arouse in lovers passions that can never be fulfilled. *Ledaean* is traditional in another way; the daughter of Leda and Zeus (see *Leda and the Swan* p.31) was Helen of Troy, whose beauty was the cause of the Trojan War. We could adopt the language of contemporary criticism and say that the beloved is a construct of the poet's writing.

To stress the traditional nature of the image of woman is to be aware of another way in which the beloved is presented. The poet casts the beloved in the role of the disdainful mistress of Renaissance love poetry, who cruelly rejects the advances of the lover. This gives Yeats' love poetry (and he is one of the great love poets of the Twentieth century) a distinctly Renaissance flavour; the poet/lover is like a courtier who observes the rituals of wooing in order to win the favours of a cool beauty who remains aloof and unpersuaded. This is given clearest expression in *Adam's Curse*, when the poet, with pride in his voice, says that he *strove* to love her *in the old high way of love* (35–6). In *He Wishes for the Cloths of Heaven* the poet, like the courtier and poet Sir Walter Raleigh, speaks of what he wants to lay beneath his beloved's feet. And he writes of the sorrows of love: *But I was young and foolish, and now am full of tears* in *Down by the Salley Gardens* (8). The ache of unfulfilment is present in *The Wild Swans at Coole*; his heart is *sore* (14), and he sees in the swans what he no longer has – *Passion* and *conquest* (23).

The sorrows of love are linked to the presentation of woman as a dominant figure. This, once more, is traditional. The happiness of the lover depends upon the beloved yielding to him; her power resides in refusal. Consequently, women are often presented as un-accountable, unpredictable and capable of making strange choices. In *A Prayer for My Daughter* Yeats talks of the capricious choices in love made by Helen of Troy and Aphrodite, adding, with an aphor-istic tang, *that fine women eat/A crazy salad with their meat* (30–1).

There are two emphases in Yeats' love poetry which are less traditional. He openly speaks of sexual passion; it is the basis of the relationship in *The Mask*, and in the rhythms of *The Cold Heaven* there is the turmoil of unsatisfied desire. In several poems sexual desire is present as an unstated theme. The Byzantium poems can be read as being about the need to escape from the torments of desire. Those poems are built around the second emphasis: sexual desire and old age. *The Living Beauty* takes the view that desire weakens, but *The Spur* and *Politics* show an old man tortured by the passions of youth. *When You Are Old* is evidence that love and old age was a theme even in Yeats' youth.

Activity

Read *No Second Troy* (p.7) and think about how the poet creates the image of woman and how he approaches the issue of love.

Discussion

The woman is presented as a figure who is superior to the age in which she is living. This accounts for the power she has over the poet. In keeping with her heroic status, she has the qualities of *nobleness* (7) and *beauty* (9). Significantly, these qualities are being presented as being made; her *nobleness* has been made *simple* (7) and her beauty is *like a tightened bow* (8). She is another Helen of Troy, with the difference that because she lives in an unheroic world of *ignorant men* (3), she has no Troy to burn. The implication may be that her true destructiveness is only evident in love; she has *filled* the poet's *days/With misery* (1–2). *Misery* is one of those surprising yet inevitable words; it seems altogether too narrow for the subject of love and yet in its expression of grinding suffering it states clearly what unrequited (unreturned) love can bring.

Yeats and His Friends

Yeats' poetry is full of people. He is in this respect like his contemporary, the English composer Edward Elgar. Elgar's *Enigma Variations* consists of musical portraits of his friends; Yeats similarly drew inspiration from his friends and names them in his poems, apart from his love poetry. We should, however, approach them in a similar way; that is, look at what he made of them in his poems. Yeats presents these figures as representative images of human qualities. Two are of particular importance – Lady Augusta Gregory and her son, Robert.

Lady Gregory (1852–1932) married into a Protestant land-owning family in the west of Ireland. Her home was Coole Park. She contributed to the revival of a distinctly Irish literary tradition by collecting folk tales and writing over forty plays. Yeats looked upon her as his encourager and patroness. In this he was reliving the Renaissance relationship between artist and patron. Coole Park becomes in his poetry the centre of a high and sophisticated culture that, in times of trouble, sustains links with the past and thereby continues to inspire artists and scholars. See *Coole Park, 1929* (p.35) (5–8), where the house and, by implication, Lady Gregory, are responsible for the creation of *Great works* (5) of art.

It may be that Yeats was keen to stress the artistic fruitfulness of Coole Park because its heir, Lady Gregory's son, Robert (1881–1918), died young. He is the subject of one of Yeats' most poised poems, *In Memory of Major Robert Gregory* (p.14), and his death is certainly the occasion for, though not necessarily the subject of, *An Irish Airman Foresees His Death* (p.18). It is interesting to question whether Robert Gregory becomes even more of a representative figure than his mother. Most of the things that are said about him in the poem that bears his name have a symbolic function: he is a keen observer of landscape (49–55), the ideal host (56), an expert horseman (57–63) and possibly, a great painter (65–9). What the poet admires (or creates?) in Gregory is a completeness which makes every element blend together in a unity: *Soldier, scholar, horseman, he,/As 'twere all life's epitome* (86–7). This is a couplet that brings home what Denis Donoghue meant by *equestrian authority*: the rhyme has the poise of the expert horseman in that because it is risky it reminds us that, to push the metaphor further, the rider is in danger of falling off, yet remains, without apparent effort, securely in the saddle. Its easy control and the comprehensive nature of Gregory's achievement – man of thought and man of action – make it an elegant summary of what Yeats valued. This is important as Yeats' presentation of his friends usually reveals something of himself.

Approaches Through Symbol and Myth

Definitions

It has been popular to approach Yeats through his use of symbols and myths, many of which arise out of his cultural background. The desire to recreate Ireland and to understand his friends and himself took, among other things, a symbolic form. To take a single example: in the Robert Gregory poem *Sidney* (47) – the Elizabethan poet, courtier and soldier who was celebrated for his courtesy – is a symbol of the range and completeness of Gregory's life.

It is wise to have a clear idea of what is meant by symbol and myth. Although there are occasions when the terms are interchangeable, a distinction can be made between them. A symbol is usually a vivid image which both points to some significance beyond itself and shares, to a limited extent, in the reality to which it points. For instance, a sunrise is a symbol of a new beginning and, at the same time, the beginning of the day. A myth is often a story (though it can also be an image) that has a representative significance for readers, who see it as revealing something important.

Because myths are often communal, their significances are related to the identity of the group, nation or religion out of which they emerge. They can also be seen, and are usually understood so by the groups who use them, as having a universal importance; King Arthur and his Knights, for instance, have become a mythical expression of the British nation and of the universal struggle of civilized behaviour against evil.

From *The Lake Isle of Innisfree* to *Under Ben Bulben* Yeats' imagination worked to use and create symbols and myths. Whatever else it might be, Innisfree is a kind of earthly paradise; the myth and symbol of a distinctly Irish Eden. The Ben Bulben poem opens with the summoning of mythical authorities such as the *Witch of Atlas* (3) and closes with the *Horseman* (94), symbol of an art that can coldly look on life and death. In the poems we may distinguish different kinds of symbol and myth.

Many of Yeats' symbols and myths are rooted in nature: fire in the eleventh stanza of *In Memory of Major Robert Gregory* is a symbol of a short but intense life; running water stands for the rhythms of life in *Easter 1916* (44); and the wind is symbolic of devastation (and possibly inspiration) in *A Prayer for My Daughter* (5). Birds are particularly prominent in Yeats. As with most symbols their significance cannot be stated exhaustively; in *The Wild Swans at Coole* the birds could be symbolic of ideal companionship, poetic inspiration and immortal souls. And, of course, they could be just birds; Yeats' images are concrete enough to be read naturalistically.

If we turn from what Yeats uses as symbols to the meaning he draws out of his symbols, we can see that art is a prominent subject: in *The Living Beauty* sculpture is used to signify art that rises above individual feeling; dance, the perfect blend of form and content, appears in *Among School Children* (57–64); song, a traditional symbol of poetry, appears in *A Prayer for Old Age* (3), and in *An Acre of Grass*, Blake (16) is used as a symbol of the imaginative artist.

Yeats used mythology from The Bible (see notes on *The Magi* on p.61), but by far his greatest debt is to Greek mythology, particularly the stories of the Trojan War. In *The Iliad* the Greek poet, Homer, gave artistic expression to the two great themes of Western literature, love and war. Yeats used the myths of Troy in *No Second*

Troy, A Prayer for My Daughter, Leda and the Swan, and *Long-Legged Fly.* As indicated above, one of the motives for this may have been personal: he had experienced one of the central features of the Trojan War – the destructiveness of love. Another pressure was Yeats' sense that he lived among a people who were unheroic, but who nevertheless needed the myths of the past in order to understand their own age. In *The Municipal Gallery Revisited* he calls on the myth of *Antaeus* (41–7) – the giant who was strong only so long as he touched the earth – to voice what he felt was the significance of what Lady Gregory, Synge, and he had done for Irish culture, by rooting it in the earthy realities of Irish life.

Issues in Yeats' Symbolism and Mythology

One of the ideas that has emerged in recent criticism is that of reflexivity. This is the notion that a writer takes as subject matter the processes of composition; in short, that art is about the making of art. Yeats was reflexive in so far as he was interested in making his poetry out of the struggles he encountered in its composition. This is the theme of *The Circus Animals' Desertion.* In another reflexive poem, *A Coat*, he explores the subject of his use of symbols and mythology. It is an attractively perky, if problematic poem. What it says is plain enough: at one time the poet made his *song a coat* (1) of *old mythologies* (3), but when his work was copied he abandoned the style and, instead, chose to walk *naked* (10). What does this mean? In his early poetic career Yeats did write long poems on Irish myths (he refers to one of them in the second stanza of *The Circus Animals' Desertion*), and later the myths figured less frequently. It could be that Yeats is simply writing about this change of emphasis, but in that case the image of nakedness might be thought inappropriate: Yeats never abandoned mythology; he was merely more sparing in its use. Another way of reading the poem is to see it as discussing the gradual move away from 'poetic' language to common speech (see Approaches pp.107–8). In that case the *old mythologies* (3) are metaphors for elaborate poetic language.

Perhaps one of the most important issues is not Yeats' use of individual myths, but his tendency to mythologize. Above it was argued that Yeats effectively mythologized his friends, turning them into

types which are representative of human qualities. When he came
to write *Leda and the Swan* (p.31) it is the actual process by which
myths come into being that is his subject. Myth, which is both
knowledge and power (13), is conceived (literally) as being generated
by the sexual union of a god (Zeus) and a woman (Leda). Written
in the immediacy of the present tense, the poem attempts to enact
the sheer mental and physical thrill of myth by using a word as
sexually explicit as *shudder* (9) and (in the manner of the cinema?)
unfolding before the reader a panorama of images drawn from the
Myths of Troy – *The broken wall, the burning roof and tower/And
Agamemnon dead* (10–11). Could Yeats be saying that the only way
to express the origin and force of myth is to use another myth?

The biggest problem with Yeats' symbols (though not necessarily
his myths) is that in addition to using traditional ones he creates
new ones. The problem is whether he can make these public enough,
so that his readers can see what they stand for. The American critic,
Theodore Spencer, put the problem in this way: *The symbols may be
too private, they may fail to communicate the emotion they represent.*
The question you should ask yourself is whether in your experience
this is true. The two Byzantium poems are a good test. The differ-
ence in *Sailing to Byzantium* (p.30) between the world of *Whatever is
begotten, born and dies* (6) and the world of the *Monuments of unage-
ing intellect* (8) establishes a traditional contrast between nature and
art that is sustained throughout the poem; but can the same be said
of the second stanza of *Byzantium* (p.38) with its *bobbin, mummy-
cloth*, and *winding path* (11–12)?

At one time it was very fashionable to approach Yeats as a
symbolist. This was in part because symbolism was a central concern
of literary critics. That emphasis is no longer strong. One of the
things you should ask yourself is whether you find it illuminating to
look at him in this way. For instance, is it more helpful than seeing
him as a dramatic poet?

Activity

Think about *Long-Legged Fly* (p.46) in the light of the discussion
above. Do you find that the symbols and myths are easy to follow, or
is Yeats being too private?

Discussion

The figures around which the poem is written are ones that are central to the literature and culture of the West. Caesar can be seen as standing for politics, Helen for the destructive power of love and Michael Angelo for art. The figures are clearly symbolic yet they are presented almost naturalistically: the noisy dog (3) and the inquisitive children (24) root these mythical beings in a world that is recognizably ours. But can the same be said of the *long-legged fly* (9, 19, 29) itself? The couplet is impressive in its mysteriousness, but you might feel that it meant something to Yeats that is not communicated to the general reader.

Approaches Through Subject Matter

Yeats' Philosophy

Yeats was a thinker who both in and outside his poetry sought to give expression to a philosophy, or world view. This is a problem, for two reasons. The first is that to many ears his philosophy sounds crazy. Yeats believed in the occult – not just automatic writing and messages from mediums (both of which he tried) – but the theory that there are patterns in history, that the future can be predicted and that astrology is the key to interpreting human personality. Many readers of Yeats must find this difficult to take.

If we are aware of Yeats' philosophy do we have to know and understand all these ideas in order to read the poetry? Yeats did do a great deal of writing about his beliefs, and many Yeats scholars have used it as a key to interpreting his poems. For instance, Yeats worked out a very complex (and rather beautiful) system about the phases of the moon and human characteristics, which critics have seized upon as a kind of 'Open Sesame' for the more difficult poems. If you want to pursue this line of thought, then a book such as Richard Ellmann's *The Identity of Yeats* is a good place to start. There is, however, an alternative approach, namely that it is not necessary to know these things in order to appreciate the poetry. The argument is similar to the one advanced about biographical criticism: since the meaning of a poem is only created by the words of the poem itself, no words from outside it can ever tell a reader what it means. From that viewpoint it does not matter what Yeats wrote elsewhere, what matters is the struggle to come to terms with the words on the page. F. R. Leavis puts the point like this: *a close critical appreciation of a successful poem of Yeats doesn't require that one should bring up any special knowledge or instructions from outside.*

There remains, however, the question of what to do with those poems that appear to refer to issues that featured in Yeats' philosophy. Two issues call for attention: gyres, and the notion of the mask. Yeats' speculations about the course of history and about how it moves in opposing phases received concrete expression in the image of the gyre – a spiral movement. This idea has a place in *The Second Coming* (p.26): *Turning and turning in the widening gyre/The falcon cannot hear the falconer* (1–2). If those lines are read in terms of the second half of the poem (9–22), then it might be correct to interpret them in terms of Yeats' notion of history moving from a phase of gentleness to one of brutality. Furthermore, those who want to read the poem politically as a prediction of communism, fascism, or the Second World War might want to emphasize Yeats' interest in theories of history. But there are other options. The image could simply be of a circling movement that spins the falcon out of reach. In that case the first eight lines might be better read as an image of universal chaos rather than a prediction based on the theory that history moves in gyres.

Yeats wrote a lot about the idea that we create public faces that protect our real selves from exposure. This is something that is done in both life and art. He called such a face a mask. As with gyres, his thinking was extensive and complex. A mask, for instance, could be very different from one's real self, and could therefore enable a person to look upon him- or herself from a different angle. A mask could also be a bridge between what a person is and what that person would like to be. But its importance to Yeats the man is a different issue from its place in the poetry. One poem is called *The Mask*; it is a teasing piece about knowledge of real identity but it does not require a theory to explain it. (If it did it would be a bad poem.) Elsewhere Yeats presents the poet as a lover, a host, a public figure, the misunderstood artist, a prophet and an old man. We could call all of these masks but, again, we would not need an elaborate theory to enable us to do so.

A final point can be made about how a reader might come to terms with Yeatsian philosophy. This is to read it all as image and metaphor; but images and metaphors of what? One suggestion is that they are about the workings of the poetic mind. Reincarnation could be read as the recurrence in the mind of images, the idea that the same motifs keep on coming back throughout a life and from generation to generation (see notes to *Under Ben Bulben* p.97). Gyres could be a way of talking about how our moods change, and masks are easily read as the way the imagination produces versions of the self. What that is saying is that one of the leading ideas in Yeats is himself; quite often poems turn out to be about his thoughts, feelings and experiences.

Yeats and Culture

We have already touched upon one of Yeats' preoccupations with culture, the responsibility of a small group – Lady Gregory, Synge, and Yeats – to preserve what is best in a world where values are under threat. The role is that of a self-appointed élite, but it is one which is performed on behalf of the whole nation – the work of the small group is the *Dream of the noble and the beggar-man* (47), in *The Municipal Gallery Revisited*. The idea that the *noble* and the *beggar* are united in their cultural aspirations is one that appeals to those ideals of organic unity – of a society that has naturally grown together – that had a deep appeal for Yeats. In rewriting Ireland he was imagining it as a country with a solid and unifying tradition.

Yeats' attempt to remake Ireland (the cultural equivalent to the political struggle for independence) was something he undertook in the consciousness that there were other cultures that had for him the status of ideals. Through his reading and travelling (some of it with Lady Gregory and her son), he came to have an absorbing interest in cultures, usually highly sophisticated ones in which the arts, including the art of living, had a central place. Two cultures particularly attracted him: Renaissance Italy and Byzantium. It is difficult to suppress the thought that Yeats hoped that Ireland could be like these. What is fairly certain is that the imagery drawn from those two cultures has a place in his poetry because he was preoccupied with understanding and remaking Ireland. Sometimes, as in *The People* (p.20), it is frustration with Ireland that summons up the image of Italy:

> I might have lived,
> And you know well how great the longing has been,
> Where every day my footfall should have lit
> In the green shadow of Ferrara wall;   (6–9)

Lived (6) might just have meant dwelt had it not been followed by *longing* (7), a word which charges *lived* with meanings of being fully alive – aware, vibrant and responsive.

In Byzantium, the capital of the Eastern Roman Empire until its conquest by the Turks in 1453, Yeats found (or created?) an image of a culture in which all aspects of life were so integrated that living became a work of art. Byzantium, moreover, was a source of images: the great dome of the cathedral, the gong, the dancing floor, and the gold image of a bird set on a golden tree glow in the two poems like the figures in *the gold mosaic of a wall* (18) in *Sailing to Byzantium*. As with Ferrara, the poet longs to be there. This longing is personal, as in *Consume my heart away* (21) from *Sailing to Byzantium*, but also communal; in the first poem the poet could be sailing from an old Ireland to one that he would like to exist, while in the second there is a strong sense of a community of craftsmen in the Emperor's smithies – an image of artists replenishing the imagination of their country?

Courtesy, Custom, and Ceremony

Inseparable from Yeats' concern with culture is his preoccupation with the manner in which people live their lives; Yeats wanted living to have the elegance of art. This, of course, is one of the reasons why he was attracted to the court life of the Renaissance. In *The Municipal Gallery Revisited* he writes of his relationship with Lady Gregory: *My medieval knees lack health until they bend* (33). As befits a Renaissance courtier poet, Yeats turns kneeling into a witty play on words: *medieval knees* suggests infirmity, and what restores them to health is being able to *bend*. But the health is not merely physical: to bend the knee in the presence of Lady Gregory is a sign of cultural good health.

The most sustained imaginative representation of the importance in life of cultivated manners and rituals is *A Prayer for My Daughter* (p.27). It is, in part, a poem about a world under threat from destructive forces. In such a world the poet prays that his daughter may have the qualities that will help her to flourish (the image of the tree is central to the poem). His most important statement is: *In courtesy I'd have her chiefly learned* (33). Yeats does not just mean good manners and politeness; the poem is about the centrality of ritual. At the close there is the image of the ideal *bridegroom* (73), who will bring her *to a house/Where all's accustomed, ceremonious* (73–4). *Accustomed* and *ceremonious* are Yeats' value words, words which embody what he thinks is of great worth – the ideal of a traditional way of life (*accustomed*) in which ritual (*ceremony*) has a normal place. He goes on to say that *custom* and *ceremony* produce what are normally thought of as natural attributes: *How but in custom and in ceremony/Are innocence and beauty born?* (77–8). The assured movement of the rhetorical question shows that the sustained practice of *custom* and *ceremony* gives birth to (the most natural of all images) two qualities which are usually thought of as entirely natural, and hence beyond the capacity of people to create – *innocence* (normally thought of as that state in which we are born) and *beauty* (a gift of nature which we cannot will into existence.) This is Yeats' version of the traditional tension between art and life, the issue as to whether what really matters is what we do (art) or what is given to us without our effort (nature). It is typical of Yeats' preoccupation with traditional culture that this idea should feature in his poetry.

Art and Impersonality

You might be alienated by the stress on *custom* and *ceremony*. Yeats seems to have had old-fashioned ideas about social behaviour, and for most people the courtly world of Irish country houses is a distant one. But it is not just a case of remote social worlds. What you might find difficult about Yeats is the artistic stance that he values. We are used to thinking that really important art is the kind that gives voice to emotions. If we can feel the pressure and swell of strong feelings, then we judge the work successful. Much of Yeats' poetry is like this; think, for instance, of the emotional turbulence of *The Cold Heaven*. Yet that poem implicitly values another kind of art, that which takes an impersonal view of life. It is there in the word *cold*. The passions of *The Cold Heaven* are anything but cold, but the word conveys the attitude of the poet to his own plight – a ruthlessly objective insight into exactly how things stand with him.

This valuing of the impersonal in art is reflected in the use of sculpture as an image of artistic endeavour. In *The Living Beauty* (p.18) the poet feels that his natural vigour is spent, so his *discontented heart* (3) (one of Yeats' chief themes) turns to beauty *that is cast out of a mould/In bronze* (3–4). The language speaks of the cold informality of art: the *beauty* is *cast* (a mechanical process) rather than shaped or fashioned; the words *mould* and *bronze* underline the rigid form and the work's hard, unyielding surface. Such art, Yeats says later, is *more indifferent to our solitude/Than 'twere an apparition* (7–8).

The hard, cold look (it has been compared to a Samurai stare) meant so much to him that he closes his 'final' poem, *Under Ben Bulben*, with the image of the horseman (remember his *equestrian authority*) *cut* (91) on *limestone quarried near the spot* (90):

Cast a cold eye
On life, on death.
Horseman, pass by!   (92–4)

Cast takes the reader back to its use in *The Living Beauty*; *cold* as the adjective qualifying *eye* (92) indicates the attitude of impersonal objectivity that Yeats valued; *life* and *death* (93) sum up the entire range of art; the *Horseman* is an image of controlled aloofness, and the final order to *pass by!* (94) encapsulates the proper indifference of art to the muddles of human emotions. Read that way, it is a concise (*cold?*) summary of what Yeats believed about art.

Activity

Read sections IV and V of *Ben Bulben* (p.49) in the light of the discussion above, and consider the place in Yeats of culture, courtesy, and impersonality.

Discussion

We see Yeats surveying the art of Egypt, Italy, England, and France in order to place the Irish in their proper context as a nation central to the European tradition; *our might* (42) is surely Ireland as well as Europe in general, and the list of names could be read as laying the foundation for the *trade* of the *Irish poets* (68). In section V, Yeats' thought about courtesy can be read as implicitly present. The ill-disciplined nature of bad poetry (a swipe at free verse?) is put down to the poets being *Base-born products of base beds* (73). Impersonality is more than implicit; the basis for their artistic greatness is *Measurement* (42), a word suggestive of the mathematical exactness of an art that transcends the turmoils of human feeling.

Poetry as a Subject

Yeats, a reflexive poet, writes poems about the writing of poems. This was not new; poets have long been fascinated with their own imaginative activity and have sought to turn this into the substance of their poetry.

In *The Circus Animals' Desertion* the poet takes stock; he begins with the search for a theme:

I sought a theme and sought for it in vain,
I sought it daily for six weeks or so   (1–2).

The words, in spite of their closeness to speech and the shrug of *or so*, have an undeniable urgency; listen, for instance, to the cumulative force of the repeated *sought*. In their muscular force, created in part by the heavy stress on *daily*, we can hear and feel the poet striving to find a theme. The lines enact the very struggles about which they speak. Yet there is a playful element appropriate to the circus in the way the lines toy with the idea that although the poet says he has no theme, the very pressure of the writing reveals that he has.

The Spur (p.43) is about the motivating power of poetry rather than its themes. Power comes from the *horrible* emotions of *lust and rage* (1). But no one is likely to find the poem itself horrible. If anything it is a merry piece; the poet playfully imagines *lust and rage* dancing *attention upon* his *old age* as if they were servants over-anxious to please, and the word *plague* (3) nicely puts them in their place as irritating hangers-on. But in the last line the poet cheerfully puts up with them; after all, he seems to say, who else has he got at his age? The point of this may be that art is always what Yeats in *Lapis Lazuli* called *gay* (3, 16, 36, 56) – brisk, vigorous, joyful and celebratory, even when the motive is far from respectable.

The business of writing is one of the concerns of *Adam's Curse*:

> 'A line will take us hours maybe;
> Yet if it does not seem a moment's thought,
> Our stitching and unstitching has been naught.   (4–6)

There is an important idea about art here. What matters in art, the lines imply, is the appearance of naturalness and ease. All art is contrived, but great art must seem as if it is entirely natural, as if it flowed from the artist apparently without effort. Yeats must surely be aware that in putting forward this artistic ideal he is inviting readers to judge him by the very standards he is advancing. If we admire the *maybe* because it has the naturalness of everyday speech, do we have the same regard for the rhyme of *naught* with *thought*? There is a feeling of rightness in the chime of the rhyme, yet *naught* might be felt to be slightly old-fashioned and therefore contrived.

Activity

Think about what the poet is saying about poetry in *The Fisherman* (p.19).

Discussion

The poet considers what it is to be a poet in relation to the society in which he finds himself. He wants to write for his *own race* (11) but finds *the reality* (12) oppressive. Consequently, he turns in *scorn of this audience* (27) to *A man who does not exist* (35) and cries (a word indicating a strong poetic outburst) that before he is old he shall have written for the imaginary fisherman

> one
> Poem maybe as cold
> And passionate as the dawn.   (38–40)

The poem clearly raises the issue of whether this poem is one that is *as cold/And passionate as the dawn.* There is certainly a cold objectivity about the way Yeats takes stock of his situation. You may wish to take the discussion further by asking whether the deft skill required by the fisherman is a metaphor for that cold art which is his ideal.

There is one more issue that is raised by Yeats' interest in writing about poetry. This is the extent to which many of his poems are essentially about poetry or, more generally, art. Many critics, for instance, think that *Byzantium* is about the actual process of artistic composition. Thus the passages about purification should be read as metaphors for the refining of artistic language, so that conventional meanings can be shed and new ones made.

Interpretation

The whole of the Approaches section has been about interpretation. To look at poems in terms of language, history, biography and themes is of course to interpret them. Yet to locate an area of interest, say, the search for a theme, is not to define the attitude that the poet takes to it. Here it is worth considering an idea about Yeats that was advanced by the critic and biographer, Richard Ellmann. His point is that whatever the subject matter, there are always two ways of reading a Yeats poem. He put it this way: *Each poem offers alternative positions.* An example will help. In *Easter 1916* (p.23) there is a symbolic passage about the stone and the stream:

> Hearts with one purpose alone
> Through summer and winter seem
> Enchanted to a stone
> To trouble the living stream.   (41–4)

The alternative positions here are that the poet is either praising those who have a single purpose or that he is showing up their limitations. These alternatives can be located in single words. The position of *alone* (41) at the end of the line singles it out for attention: does it indicate a romantic and even heroic solitariness or the fate of those who, because they do not change, are isolated from *the living stream* (44)? The same kind of thing can be said of *Enchanted* (43): does it mean a magical transformation, or a bewitchment?

Activity

Is it possible to have different readings of the third stanza of *September 1913* (p.10)?

Discussion

How should *delirium* and *brave* (22) be read? If we emphasize *derilium*, then the figures from the past will appear to be deluded and even slightly crazed, but if the word *brave* is stressed, then they will appear to be heroic martyrs, and *delirium* might indicate not derangement but a state of rapture.

This way of interpreting Yeats is attractive but it is not without drawbacks. There is, first of all, the issue of whether it is true of *all* his poems. The second problem is whether it suggests that Yeats is indecisive. This is certainly not how he sounds to me; if several meanings are present, I think it is wiser to regard Yeats as either bracing himself in the face of complexity or see him playfully sporting with the multiple meanings his poetry has generated. It is also essential to ask whose voice we hear. Sometimes we hear the poet speak as in *Easter 1916*, but in other poems we must remember that a specially created voice (or mask) is present.

Yeats' Thought

We must distinguish between Yeats' philosophy and his thought. His philosophy is his ideas – the notion that history runs in gyres or that the soul is reincarnated – whereas his thought is the way he went about thinking, his attitude and mental processes. Another way of putting it is to say that his thought is the cast of his mind, the channels into which his thinking flowed.

The first thing to be said about the way Yeats thinks is that he is increasingly preoccupied with the actual processes of thought rather than the ideas. (Some readers have claimed that one of the drawbacks of Yeats is that he is short on ideas.) The boldest statement of this is in *The Circus Animals' Desertion*: *Players and painted stage took all my love,/And not those things that they were emblems of* (31–2). Neither *players* nor *painted stage* is the subject matter, but subject matter is of

no interest to Yeats; what absorbs him is the actual processes of art –
how the meanings are made, not what the meanings are.

Related to this concern with the processes of art is an emphasis
upon the power of the creative imagination. In this respect Yeats
seems strikingly modern, because his stress is on how we create
rather than discover meanings. Yeats said: *The world knows nothing
because it has made nothing, we know everything because we have made
everything*. In *The Municipal Gallery Revisited* (p.44) the pictures are
said to be of *'an Ireland/The poets have imagined, terrible and gay'* (11–
12). We are on modern ground here. One of the most insistent
stresses in contemporary thinking is that people devise rather than
discover meanings. Sense, significance and even truth are held to be
our own constructs, and therefore our supposed picture of the world
is one that we have made, and a study of it will reveal not 'reality'
but the way in which we think, feel and imagine. In *The Municipal
Gallery Revisited* the imagining is multiple; Yeats imagines the Irish
painters bringing Ireland into existence through an act of the imag-
ination. And the Ireland imagined is itself imaginative, because it
has the dramatic qualities of tragedy (*terrible*) and comedy (*gay*).
The point about Yeats is that he not only imagined but made the
act of imagining one of his themes.

Another prominent element in his thinking which is modern is
the stress on change. Traditional thinkers stress continuity and
stability; radicals, on the other hand, insist that all is subject to
change. The heady impact of change underlies *The Second Coming*;
things spin out of control and the centre can no longer *hold* (3)
them together. What is remarkable about Yeats' presentation of
such tumultuous change is that it thrills him with joy. *Lapis Lazuli*
(p.41) is a poem in which the rhythms exhilaratingly enact an
unquenchable joy in face of the certainty that all things will perish.
There is a rumbustious pleasure in *Pitch like King Billy bomb-balls
in/Until the town lies beaten flat* (7–8). The 'creed' of the poem is one
that blithely accepts loss and rejoices in creativity: *All things fall and
are built again,/And those that build them again are gay* (35–6).

Awareness of change lies at the base of another twentieth-century
emphasis, relativity. People have become less sure of absolutes, of
dependable, unchanging certainties, and aware that meanings are

the products of differing perspectives. This has led some people to think that if all thought is a matter of perspective, there can be no final or ultimate truth, and that thinking will always be an unful-filled movement towards an unattainable goal. If there is no final truth, there can be no arrival and no rest. Yeats' sympathy for this view makes *The Magi* one of his most radical poems. He deliberately chooses the Christmas story – a story that has represented the absolute for millions of people – and turns the wise men into searchers who have been enticed, but not satisfied by what they have found on *the bestial floor* (8). Yeats has moved them away from the stabilities of Christian meaning into a world where they are *unsatisfied* (2, 7) and so can only – *Now as at all times* (1) – search.

Activity

Read *Death* (p.35) in the light of the discussion above and ask your-self how characteristic it is of Yeats' thought.

Discussion

Animals are incapable of either *dread* or *hope* (1), because, as animals, they cannot see the world in terms that would enable them to feel that way. Only man *awaits his end/Dreading and hoping all* (3–4). The quality of *A great man* (7) is that he can rise above fear. In the words *Casts derision* (9), there is the hint that in the same way in which a sculptor creates by casting his work in metal, so people can make themselves. At the climax of this short poem about the human capacity to create, the poet asserts that *Man has created death* (12). In the context of the poem it is clear that this means that all death stands for is something that is the product of human thinking.

A consideration of Yeats' thought brings these Approaches to a fitting conclusion, since it highlights one of the most intriguing things about Yeats – the blending in his work of the traditional and the distinctly modern. Yeats steeped himself in the cultures of the past, and yet he understood them in modern ways. This is why he matters; he stands in the tradition of poets going back to Homer and does all that we expect of a traditional poet, and at the same time he knows what it is to live in the modern world. The very remarkable thing about Yeats is that his buoyancy in the face of what he finds in the world is abundant and undiminished. And this is not because he is without care or concern; the life of the mind and the making of beautiful things are what he feels passionately about, and moreover, these things matter to him so much that he struggles with the disciplines of poetry – the right words in the right order – to turn them into the *excited reverie* (13) in A *Prayer for My Daughter* of art. Above all, whatever his subject, he joyfully sings. When we first hear him and when we are better acquainted with his work, we are held and delighted by Yeats' voice.

Chronology

1865   Yeats born in Dublin on 13 June into a traditionally Protestant family and into a country that was not an independent nation but part of the United Kingdom. He was given the Christian names William Butler, Butler being one of his mother's family names

1867   Yeats family move to London to enable his father, Jack, to work as a painter

1868   Spends the first of many summers with his mother's family in Sligo, a County in the west of Ireland

1872   Yeats' mother and the children settle in Sligo

1874   Family returns to London

1879   Family moves to Bedford Park, a garden suburb in West London noted for its artistic residents

1881   Financial difficulties mean the family return to Dublin

1884   Yeats enrols in a Dublin Art School

1885   Begins to publish; meets John O'Leary, the scholar and Irish patriot who comes to epitomize for Yeats all that is best in Irish Nationalism; his interest in the occult finds expression in his founding of the Dublin Hermetic Society

1887   Family comes back to London, where Yeats furthers his interests in the occult

1889   Meets Maud Gonne on 30 January – an actress with a passionate devotion to Irish Nationalism. His first books of poetry *The Wanderings of Oisin and Other Poems* and *Crossways*

1891   Proposes for the first time to Maud Gonne. In the manner of a medieval suitor he writes poems about her and continues to press her to accept him for the next twelve years

1892   First performance of Yeats' play *The Countess Cathleen*, a work he began in 1889, no doubt as a response to meeting Maud Gonne

1893   *The Rose* is published

1894   Yeats continues to live in both London and Dublin. He goes to Paris, where he moves in literary and occult circles

1895   Yeats' first collection is published

1896   Meets J. M. Synge, a poet and playwright from a Protestant background. Having recently visited them himself, Yeats suggests that Synge goes to the Arran Isles for subject matter and inspiration. See *In Memory of Major Robert Gregory* (p.14)

1897   Visits Coole Park, to discuss with Lady Gregory the establishment of a distinctly Irish theatre

1898   Delivers a patriotic speech at a dinner to mark the centenary of the death of Wolfe Tone

1899   *The Wind Among the Reeds* is published

1902   Maud Gonne plays the title role in Yeats' play *Cathleen N' Houlihan*

1903   Maud Gonne marries the Irish Nationalist John MacBride

1904   Opening of the Abbey Theatre in Dublin, an essential element in Yeats' and Lady Gregory's campaign to establish an authentically Irish theatrical tradition; several of his plays are performed there, both in 1904 and in subsequent years; *In the Seven Woods* is published

1905   Yeats becomes involved in the plans of Hugh Lane to build an art gallery in Dublin to house his collection of French Impressionists; Irish authorities refuse, and the pictures go to the National Gallery in London; Yeats sees this as an example of how uncivilized Dublin (and Ireland) is, a view that later finds expression in *September 1913* (p.10) and *The People* (p.20)

1907   Visits Italy with Lady Gregory and her son, Robert. In Ravenna he sees mosaics in the style of Byzantium; death of John O'Leary – see the refrain of *September 1913* (p.10)

1909   Death of J. M. Synge

1910   *The Green Helmet and Other Poems* is published; Yeats accepts a small pension from the British Government

1914   *Responsibilities* published; the British Government agrees to Home Rule for Ireland, but enactment of the law is delayed because of political problems in Europe; The First World War begins (1914–1918)

1915   Yeats is offered, but refuses, a knighthood

1916   The Easter Rising: Patrick Pearse and an army of volunteers take over the Dublin Post Office, and from there proclaim Irish independence; the Rising attracts little support until the British begin executing the leaders; John MacBride is amongst those who are shot; Yeats' response is *Easter 1916*

1917   Yeats buys the Norman Tower near the Coole Park estate and names it Thoor Ballylee. *The Wild Swans at Coole* is published; Yeats marries Georgie Hyde-Lees; in Russia the Bolsheviks seize power

1918   In the last year of the First World War, Robert Gregory dies while serving with the Royal Flying Corps in Italy, see *In Memory of Major Robert Gregory* (p.14) and *An Irish Airman Foresees His Death* (p.18); in the General Election seventy-three Sinn Fein candidates are elected but refuse to take up their Westminster seats; they set up an alternative Assembly, called the 'Dail' in Dublin

1919   The 'Troubles' begin; for two years the IRA fight an independent campaign; in 1921 the 'Dail' recognizes the IRA as the effective army of the new Ireland; Yeats' daughter Anne is born, see *A Prayer for My Daughter* (p.27)

1921   *Michael Robartes and the Dancer* is published

1922   Civil War breaks out in Ireland when the Irish Free State accepts the partition of Ireland into Ulster (still part of the United Kingdom) and the Free State in the south; fighting occurs near the Tower; Yeats becomes a Senator of the Irish Free State; Mussolini forms a government in Italy, in the next three years he outlaws other political parties

1923   Yeats is awarded the Nobel Prize for Literature

1925   Travels to Italy; visits abroad, particularly in Winter, are to become a feature of his life

1927   Assassination of Kevin O'Higgins, the Irish Minister of Justice who had insisted upon a firm line against irregulars who carried guns, see *Death* (p.35); Yeats' health is poor, in the coming years he is to suffer from lung and heart problems

1928   *The Tower* is published

1932   The death of Lady Gregory, see *Coole Park, 1929* (p.35) and *Coole Park and Ballylee, 1931* (p.37); Yeats moves to Riversdale, near Dublin; Riversdale is the setting for *An Acre of Grass* (p.43)

1933   *The Winding Stair and Other Poems* is published

1935   *Parnell's Funeral and Other Poems* is published

1936   Spanish Civil War begins; in England it is seen as an opportunity for politically active people to fight against (and, in a few cases, for) fascism, see *Politics* (p.48)

1937   Yeats makes a number of radio broadcasts for the BBC

1938   *New Poems* is published

1939   Death of Yeats in the south of France on 28 January; he is buried in France; *Last Poems* is published; in September the Second World War begins; Ireland remains neutral

1948   Yeats' body reburied in the churchyard at Drumcliff, see *Under Ben Bulben* (p.49)

Further Reading

Editions

Collected Poems of W. B. Yeats (Macmillan, 1936) contains the complete poetic works and is available in hardback and paperback. Macmillan also published a small selection of the poems with brief notes, edited by A. Norman Jeffares.

Collected Poems, ed. Daniel Albright (Everyman, 1990) probably the best critical edition giving detailed notes.

Biography

Richard Ellman, *Yeats: the Man and the Mask* (Faber and Faber, 1973) established now as the classic text on Yeats' life.

A. Norman Jeffares, *W. B. Yeats* (Hutchinson, 1988) provides the most recent biography.

Jon Stallworthy, *Between the Lines: Yeats' Poetry in the Making* (Clarendon Press, 1965) offers some intriguing insights into Yeats' drafting of his poetry.

Criticism

The following introductions to Yeats' work are recomended:

Denis Donoghue, *W. B. Yeats* in *The Fontana Modern Masters* series (Fontana, 1971) provides an excellent authoritative introduction.

A. Norman Jeffares ed., *W. B. Yeats* in *The Critical Heritage* series (Routledge and Kegan Paul, 1977) contains some fascinating early criticism of the poetry.

Edward Malins, *A Preface to Yeats* (Longman, 1974) also gives information on the life.

Peter Ure, *W. B. Yeats* (Oliver and Boyd, 1963) offers sound criticism of the poetry.

More detailed criticism will be found in:

Harold Bloom, *Yeats* (Oxford University Press, 1970) favours the early poems in its comments over the later ones.

Richard Ellman, *The Identity of Yeats* (Faber and Faber, 1964) is still much used.

Seamus Heaney, *Preoccupations* (Faber and Faber, 1980) gives the views of a contemporary Irish poet.

F. R. Leavis, *Lectures in America* – essay (Chatto and Windus, 1969) provides a brilliant analysis of the Byzantium poems.

David Pierce, *W. B. Yeats* in *The State of the Art* series (Bristol Press, 1989) offers interesting ideas about the current work of scholars and critics.

W. W. Robson, *A Prologue to English Literature* (Batsford, 1986) gives brief but illuminating general comments.

John Unterecker, *A Reader's Guide to W. B. Yeats* (Thames and Hudson, 1975) is still widely used.

Ivor Winters, *The Poetry of W. B. Yeats* (Alan Swallow, 1960) gives a hostile view of the poetry.

Tasks

1 Consider the voice in *The Municipal Gallery Revisited*. Can it be described as lofty, noble, and authoritative, or is it merely the pose of a braggart? Try reading some of the other poems with this issue in mind.

2 In the light of the discussion in the Word Order section of Approaches (pp.104–6), think about the effectiveness of the rhetorical strategies in *Among School Children*.

3 Read *September 1913*, *Sailing to Byzantium* and *Lapis Lazuli* and see if any words have the Yeatsian qualities of precision, surprise and inevitability.

4 Read *Adam's Curse*, *The Wild Swans at Coole*, *In Memory of Major Robert Gregory*, and *Under Ben Bulben*, and explore how their meanings and impacts are acted out in the stanza form, the rhymes and the line lengths.

5 By looking at the words he uses, consider how Yeats creates his picture of Ireland in *Pardon, Old Fathers*, *Coole Park, 1929*, *Coole Park and Ballylee, 1931*, and *The Municipal Gallery Revisited*.

6 How in *Easter 1916* does Yeats present the complexities of politics, and the sense that the texture of the nation's life has changed? Do you think that he makes the events universal enough to be of interest to non-Irish readers?

7 Do you find that in his love poems Yeats is too tied to traditional ideas about the roles of men and women, and too preoccupied with his own sorrows? You may like to consider *No Second Troy*, *The Cold Heaven*, *The Wild Swans at Coole*, *A Deep-Sworn Vow*, *To a Young Girl*, and *A Prayer for My Daughter*.

8 In *The Municipal Gallery Revisited* Yeats says *my glory was I had such friends* (55). What does Yeats make of his friends in that poem, and in *In Memory of Major Robert Gregory*? You may also ask whether he sees his friends chiefly as giving him glory.

9 Consider the importance of both the Trojan War and Greek mythology in Yeats' poems. You might think about whether it is helpful to approach these issues in biographical, cultural or artistic terms.

10 Is Yeats successful in making his ideal cultures attractive to the reader? *The People, Coole Park, 1929, Coole Park and Ballylee, 1931*, and *Byzantium* may be considered.

11 Is it helpful to read Yeats' poems as being essentially about the problem of the artist, irrespective of the apparent subject of each poem? Useful poems to read are *Adam's Curse, In Memory of Major Robert Gregory, An Irish Airman Foresees His Death*, and *Byzantium*.

12 Trace the basic elements in Yeats' thought – the role he gives to the creative imagination, the presence of change, and the relativity of all ideas – as they appear in *Under Ben Bulben*.

13 Make a selection of ten poems which, in your view, embody the chief characteristics of Yeats' art and thought. It may help to write an account of the reasons for your choice.

14 Choose one poem by Yeats and read it carefully so that you are in touch with the changes in rhythm, pace, level of feeling, and intellectual engagement. Once you have done this, try reading the poem aloud to bring out all the changes of which you have become aware.

15 It is sometimes said that Yeats' short poems are more interesting than his longer ones. Consider the qualities of *To a Young Girl, A Deep-Sworn Vow*, and *The Spur*. Do you find them more impressive than, say, *Under Ben Bulben*?

16 It has been argued that what matters in Yeats is not what he has to say but the power of his assertions, and the conviction with which he speaks. Test out this idea by reading the two poems about Byzantium.

Yeats as a young man: the pose is suggestive of the dreamy and Romantic
air of early poems, such as *The Lake Isle of Innisfree* (p.2) and *He Wishes for
The Cloths of Heaven* (p.4)

Maud Gonne: this photo brings out something of the determined and
independent spirit of the one who was to Yeats *the loveliest woman born* (see
A Prayer for My Daughter p.27)

The ruins of the Dublin Post Office after the Easter Rising in 1916. The prophetic note in *Easter 1916* (p.23) – A *terrible beauty is born* – is interestingly at odds with the amount of debris in evidence

The imposing presence of Ben Bulben may have suggested to Yeats the quality of *indomitable Irishry* which he celebrates in *Under Ben Bulben* (p.49)

Facing page top

The Norman Tower at Ballylee. The setting for *In Memory of Major Robert Gregory* (p.14) and the Coole Park poems (see p.35 and p.37)

Facing page bottom

Lady Augusta Gregory, appropriately photographed as if she were a Renaissance patroness (see p.117)

Yeats in old age: *A foolish passionate man* (*A Prayer for Old Age* p.40) or *An old man's eagle mind* (*An Acre of Grass* p.43)

148

Index of Titles and First Lines